ULTIMATE DISASTER PREP & PLANNING HANDBOOK

SHTF PREPPING, BUG IN, BUG OUT, STOCKPILE & HOME DEFENSE GUIDE

By

Robbie J. Jones

Published by:

CSB Academy Publishing Company.
P.O. Box 966
Semmes, Alabama 36575

Cover & Interior designed
By
Angie Anderson

First Edition

Table of Contents

FOREWORD

> As of January 2015, California has declared a state of emergency as it enters its 4th year of severe drought.

> The world power grid is vulnerable to an EMP attack, and the US power grid is so old that it can potentially collapse on its own.

> US debt is $18.3 trillion, which means the dollar could collapse at any time.

> Riots and unrest are spreading throughout the world.

> Rise of active shooter situations worldwide.

> Earthquakes throughout the world have increased in magnitude and frequency.

> Severe weather storms like tsunamis, hurricanes, tornadoes and typhoons are increasingly more common.

> The nuclear war threats have been on the rise.

> Global terrorism is reaching a new level of uncertainty.

What do all of these events have in common? Why am I giving you these facts? I'm not trying to scare anyone, but rather raise awareness. All of these events, and others not listed here, can lead to either a local or a global catastrophe at a moment's notice. The chances of even a small event occurring in your area are increasing every day, and most people simply aren't aware of these facts or feel they don't affect them.

However, I now ask you another question. Are you prepared? Have you prepared yourself and your home for a local or global catastrophic event? Even if you haven't prepared, would you know what to do in the event that something happened? Consider just a few more facts.

➢ A single individual requires a gallon of safe drinking water a day to survive.

➢ The average household only has about a day to three days' worth of food on hand.

➢ The average grocery store only has three weeks' worth of food in stock.

➢ The average local response time for disaster assistance is a week or more.

Armed with these facts, would you be able to survive until assistance arrives? What if assistance never came as a result of a global collapse? Again, these facts aren't meant to scare you, but rather to make you aware of something. While there is a chance you may never face a dire situation in your area, there are still many benefits you can get from being prepared for a disaster.

In this book, I'm going to teach you how to get started with disaster preparation. Folks, this is not rocket science; it's a process you have to be aware of and follow. I'm going to show you how everyone in a family, including those who are disabled, can be prepared for any disaster.

We'll go into detailed specifics on how you can prepare yourself and your home. Best of all, I'll show you how you can prepare on a budget, so no matter what your household situation and financial means are, you will be able to get prepared. This will give you an advantage over others when a disaster occurs in your area.

When I taught disaster survival, I always told people that preparation is not all about stockpiling food and water and securing a shelter. Well, think about it, if you only need to take shelter and hide for a week, then it is fine to just have food, water, and a secure shelter. But what if the disaster is longer-lasting? Would you be okay with just those three items? Or would you need to have a few more things to survive in the long run?

Ideally, to me, disaster preparation is much more than just that; true preparation means learning a few basic survival skills, mastering them, practicing them and becoming a pro at them. To be truly successful, you need to take a comprehensive approach and look at the broader picture, and that is exactly what I have done in this book.

A true survivor is a person who knows how to survive in any situation and make the best out of it. A true survivor knows how to find food, water, or shelter when there is none. A true survivor knows how to handle emergencies when there is no 911 service available.

Any book on this topic can show you what and how to stockpile food, but that is just a small part of survival training; a big part of that training is learning which skills you will need, what to learn, what to use and how to use them.

My disaster survival course was taught in 3 separate segments. First, I taught and demonstrated what disaster preparation truly is, as I show you in this book.

Next, I taught them which gears they need and how to use them most effectively; third, I taught them what to do during and after a major disaster. These three books are essentially the notes I followed when I taught "Disaster Survival," and so far, I have successfully taught 17 groups of people in 5 different countries.

THE BASICS OF PREPPING

Before you can get started prepping, it is important to first consider what type of event you want to prepare for in your area. There are numerous small and large-scale events that can occur in your area or even in your country.

You can't be prepared for every single event, but you can be prepared for those most likely to occur in your area. There are three categories of events. Let's consider them, so you know what is most likely to occur in your area.

3 TYPES OF DISASTERS

CATEGORY C: SMALL-SCALE CRITICAL EVENTS

> Car crashes (37,000 die in the US a year, and nearly 2 million are injured)

- Rape (nearly 300,000 sexual assaults are reported in the US every year)

- Firearm assaults (1.1 million were reported in the US in 2013)

- Electric shocks (200 people a year are sent to the emergency room)

- Drowning (3,500 die a year, that's ten per day)

- Food poisoning (1 in 6 people in the US get sick a year, and 3,000 die)

- Heart attacks (leading cause of death in the US, with over 600,000 a year)

- Rapid dog attacks (40,000 are treated for rabies in the US every year)

- Carbon monoxide poisoning (500 deaths a year and 15,000 reported cases)

- House fires (1.2 million a year in the US)

- Hiking accidents (200,000 people a year are hospitalized in the US each year)

- Boating accidents (300 deaths a year in the US)

- Weather-related deaths (2,000 a year in the US alone, most from cold-related issues)

- Home invasions (will affect one in five homes at some point)

CATEGORY B: MEDIUM-SCALE DISASTERS

➢ Terrorist attacks (13,463 global attacks in 2014; 32,700 deaths)

➢ Flash floods (100 US deaths a year)

➢ Earthquakes (over 1,300 with a magnitude 5 or higher occur each year globally)

➢ Volcanic eruptions (the US alone has 169 active volcanoes)

➢ Tsunamis

➢ Wildfire (in 2014, the US had 63,000 total fires that burned 3.6 million acres)

➢ Ice storms (15 happen a year in the US)

➢ Riots (lately, we are seeing a lot of these breaking out throughout the country)

➢ Avalanches

➢ Chemical spills

➢ Drought

➢ Prolonged power grid down situations

➢ Snowstorms and blizzards

➢ Heat waves

➢ Mudslides and landslides

➢ Radiation leaks

- ➢ Localized martial law

- ➢ Hurricanes

CATEGORY A: LARGE-SCALE DEVASTATING EVENTS

- ➢ Nuclear attacks

- ➢ War

- ➢ Viruses

- ➢ Pandemics

- ➢ Mega-drought

- ➢ Economic Collapse

- ➢ Food crisis

- ➢ Natural or man-made EMP disasters

- ➢ Collapse of society

- ➢ Asteroid strike

While it is unlikely a Category A disaster will happen, there is always that possibility. However, just consider the list and numbers associated with events in Categories B and C. That is a lot of reasons to get prepared, since you are likely to experience at least a few in your area in your lifetime.

Consider that, as of 2016, within the last ten years, there have been 699 major disasters declared in the US alone.

That's at least 70 a year. This doesn't even account for incidents on the Category C list.

So now that you see why disaster preparation is so important, let's get into exactly what it entails.

WHAT IS PREPPING

In its simplest form, prepping is basically about preparing for the future. Since there is no certainty about the future, those who prepare are essentially preparing for the worst while hoping for the best. The concept of prepping is also fairly simple.

The goal of prepping is to maintain a specific standard of living to protect against disaster. Prepping is a way to build a defense against realistic calamities, such as illness and accidents, rather than massive crises. Those who choose to prepare are simply ordinary people who agree to live by specific principles.

THE 7 PRINCIPLES OF PREPPING

For the disaster preparer, several principles are involved. By doing these things, they are adequately prepared for most incidents in their area. Consider these principles to get a good idea of what is involved in disaster preparation.

STOCKPILING NECESSARY SUPPLIES

Everyone needs at least water, food, and shelter to survive. In addition, during a long-term disaster or survival situation, individuals need a continual supply of these three things. Prepares know this and try to be prepared should a disruption in these supplies occur. They do this by stocking up on extra food or by growing their own garden.

LEARNING IMPORTANT SKILLS

True disaster preparation goes beyond storing food, water, and other emergency supplies; it involves regularly learning and practicing survival skills. There are plenty of things you can learn on your own at home or by taking courses.

For example, you can learn outdoor cooking methods, emergency first aid, hunting, fishing or shelter building. The specific skills you learn will depend on where you live and what situations you are likely to face after a disaster occurs in your area.

BUILDING A COMMUNITY

Those who prepare for a disaster realize the importance of getting to know others with similar mindsets. You can learn from each other and help out if a disaster should happen. There is a chance you won't be ready before a disaster occurs.

But if you know of some people (friends or neighbors) who have done their preparation, then you can pool your skills and resources and work as a close-knit community or as a team where you contribute your skills and the "know-how" and survive the disaster.

THRIFTINESS AND FRUGALITY

Disaster preparation involves reducing waste by focusing on living within one's means. Prepares to look for ways to be more efficient with their time and money. This doesn't mean living off the land every day, but just being more prudent in how money is used and keeping in mind when the next paycheck comes.

INDEPENDENCE

There are many forms of independence. You may want to get out of debt and gain control over your money to achieve financial independence. Perhaps you want personal independence from addictions to things such as alcohol or drugs. Each individual has a personal view of independence, and preparing for a disaster can help teach and support individuals in achieving it.

INDUSTRIOUSNESS

Those who prepare for disasters are always looking for ways to improve their learning skills by exploring and undertaking various tasks. They are aware that success requires hard work. They are industrious in getting things done rather than relying on others.

SELF-RELIANCE

Self-reliance requires an individual to provide for their own needs through their own skills and on-hand resources. Everyone should learn how to garden, repair, and fix things, so they don't have to rely on others. This means working with your own hands to provide your own goods and services, which also helps you save money in the long run.

WHAT IF NO DISASTER EVER HAPPENS

All this preparation and skills seem like a lot of work and time. So, what happens if you do all this and no major disaster ever happens in your area? It is always best to be prepared for the worst, but hope for the best. At a minimum, you will be more relaxed and at ease knowing you are secure in the event of a catastrophic situation. However, let's look at some of the many benefits you can get from disaster preparation, even if the big one never happens.

8 KEY BENEFITS OF PREPPING

While there are many benefits to disaster preparedness, many people still feel it is a waste of time. In today's society, people want to see immediate results; rather than spending time and effort to see the actual accomplishment. Plus, there is a lot of misinformation out there about disaster preparation, which has led to confusion and arguments.

The only way you can have the motivation to prepare is to find a benefit or reason to prepare that affects you. To help with this, I've put together a comprehensive list of disaster-preparation benefits.

Take the time to read this list and think about your life. You are likely to find at least a few of these benefits as reasons to start prepping. Many of these benefits can be enjoyed in regular life, even if a major disaster never happens.

SAVE MONEY

I put this at the top because I feel this is one of the benefits that will attract many. In general, it is wise to save money for the future, but disaster preparedness will help you take it a step further. When you stock up for disaster preparation, you will have more items on hand, so you can use your stock while waiting for things to go on sale and never have to pay full price for anything.

Disaster preparation can even include off-the-grid living, saving you money on groceries, electricity, water and other utilities. There are also a number of do-it-yourself projects that will save you money on buying things. Lastly, in today's struggling economy, you never know when a loss of a job may happen and when you have money and supplies stockpiled, you can use them while you take the time to look for another job.

REDUCE WASTE

We live in a throwaway society. If something is a little old, outdated or no longer serves its stated purpose, we just throw it away and buy something new. This isn't to say you should become a hoarder and hold on to everything. However, a disaster preparer knows when something has an additional purpose or use, so they hold on to it and give it new life rather than filling the landfills.

IMPROVED PHYSICAL FITNESS

While disaster preparation may not help you get fit specifically, it can help you stay in shape. There are a number of preparation skills, such as gardening, chopping wood, hunting and more, that will help you stay in shape if you do them regularly.

You will also be improving your health by eating healthier and growing your own food. So, in addition to maintaining physical fitness, you will also maintain a healthier lifestyle. We'll talk more about fitness later in this book.

FINANCIAL PROTECTION

At some point, inflation drives up prices for common food and household goods. When you have items stockpiled, you can protect yourself against inflation. Even if a global or national financial crisis never happens, that doesn't mean we haven't seen a depression or a recession. When you prepare before things get bad, you will have protection against serious damage to you and your family.

PREPARATION FOR SMALL DISASTERS

A disaster doesn't have to be big to cause damage. You have no way to prevent natural disasters such as floods or earthquakes, but you can prepare yourself and your family for the worst. Then there are smaller disasters, such as house fires and power outages. When you are prepared, you can reduce the damaging effects of these events.

SMOOTHER EVACUATION

We've all seen the clogged roads and panicked effects that happen during an evacuation. What would you do in this situation? How soon and how easily can you evacuate? When you are prepared, you can leave quickly, knowing you have everything you need, and not get stuck in the crowd as they scramble to prepare and leave.

PREPARING FUTURE GENERATIONS

Even if you feel a disaster won't be likely in your lifetime, what about your children and later generations? Within the last ten years alone, it is easy to see that natural and man-made disasters are worsening and occurring with greater frequency. When you start preparing for disasters now, you can pass along valuable skills and knowledge to your kids and grandkids who may actually need to be prepared for a major disaster or two.

LESS STRESS

With so many problems today, it is easy to become stressed or overwhelmed. Especially if things seem beyond your control, preparing for potential disasters can take some of the stress away from your life. Not only will it make you feel more protected, but you'll also know you are prepared for even minor incidents or emergencies.

Now that you have examined the benefits and reasons to be prepared, you're likely more inclined to get started. Before you go out and start stockpiling, there are a few things you need to consider.

6 ITEMS TO CONSIDER BEFORE YOU START PREPPING

While it is possible to simply start building your stockpile and preparing for a disaster, it is also important to consider your individual situation before you begin. There are six things to think about and take into consideration before you begin disaster preparation:

1) Your age and how it impacts your physical health.

2) Your sex and how it impacts your ability to do certain physical activities, such as self-defense.

3) Your family and whether or not they have the same view as you when it comes to disaster preparation.

4) Your location will determine the best disaster to prepare for first.

5) Your financial situation will determine how much preparation you can do and what you should stockpile first.

6) Your medical conditions and what you may need to stay prepared for these in a disaster situation.

ARE YOU MENTALLY PREPARED FOR A DISASTER?

When you find yourself in a disaster situation, the right tools and skills can make a big difference. However, knowledge and equipment alone will not help you survive if you don't have the mental toughness to handle the situation. Your brain is often the most important tool of all when it comes to disaster survival.

Having skills and knowledge will only get you so far if you don't know how to react to a situation where life and death depend on the choices you make.

History is filled with everyday people who have survived horrific conditions even without survival gear or specialized skills. On the other hand, there have also been individuals with specific training and tools who have died in survival situations. The dividing factor seems to be whether people are mentally prepared to do what it takes to survive the circumstances.

Choosing to survive first involves avoiding the *victim mindset*. When you have a victim mindset, you won't be able to look for ways to survive with whatever you have on hand. A **survival mindset** means you can adapt to any situation and keep going no matter what happens. Mental toughness means you can stay in control of your fear and anxiety during a survival situation.

When you find yourself in a disaster, your first inclination should be to stop and assess the circumstances, even if your mind is telling you to panic. There are many ways our bodies may react to fear, but you want to avoid the two extremes. First, you don't want to let your fear get the worst of you, so you aren't able to make wise decisions. Second, you don't want to let your fear lead you to make hasty, ill-considered decisions that make the situation worse.

There are a few things you can do to help develop the mental toughness you need to survive disaster situations. Consider the following three tips (If you self-analyze and practice these tips long enough, you can actually increase your mental strength).

1. **Positive Attitude.** When you have a positive attitude, you won't suffer from self-pity; instead, you will use tough circumstances as stepping stones toward a solution. Those who have a positive attitude will respond rather than react.

2. **Manage Emotions.** Pay attention to how you react in stressful or fearful everyday situations. Then practice managing these emotions, and if needed, use relaxation techniques, deep breathing or any other method that works for you.

3. **Watch Your Ego.** Rather than thinking that a disaster will never happen to you, start to recognize that something can happen, and you should be prepared for it. Survival preparation and training will improve your self-confidence while keeping you grounded with realities.

Now that you've considered what you need to do to be prepared, let's get started on the important things. Let's look at how you can get started with prepping.

HOW TO START PREPPING

The best way to approach disaster preparation is through a series of steps and layers. You first need to determine your unique situation based on the six things you considered above in the previous segment. Then you can start your layered approach and start building up how many days, weeks, months and years you are going to be prepared for.

The last thing you will need to consider before you start preparing is whether you should *bug in* or *bug out* during a disaster. Bugging in means you will stay inside your home until the situation is resolved, and bugging out means you are leaving your home and possibly your city to find safety elsewhere. In my humble opinion, you should be prepared for both.

In city living, it can be best to bug in for smaller disasters, but if a larger disaster hits and the city is no longer livable, you will need to bug out to a safer location. Most preparation steps apply to both situations, but make sure to consider both when deciding how to store your supplies.

WHO CAN PREPARE?

There is, unfortunately, a lot of misconceptions about disaster preparation thanks to mainstream media. The majority of people who prepare are everyday individuals who simply want to be better equipped to deal with the uncertainty around us in our daily lives.

WHAT DOES IT TAKE?

Being prepared will require three things:

1. The skills to be self-reliant and able to deal with a variety of situations.

2. A plan to deal with potential problems. It should be flexible enough to handle unknown factors that may arise.

3. Appropriate equipment, gear, and supplies to help support your plan and improve your skills. Planning ahead and having gear is helpful and makes survival easier, but you should always know how to survive on your own skills.

DISASTER PREPARATION MYTHS

As I said earlier, mainstream media has given many people a wrong view of what disaster preparation is and who does it. Let me take a moment to correct some of the myths that surround disaster preparation.

Disaster preparation doesn't mean you need to have a weapon or ammunition in your home. Having any form of weapons training is a personal choice, and some choose not to pursue it. If you are trained and know how to use a firearm properly, then my advice is to have a good supply of ammunition and store it safely and securely.

Those who prepare for disasters don't have to believe the world is going to end tomorrow. Rather, they are simply people who want to be more self-reliant.

The disaster preparation community isn't made up of angry loners. Rather, you will find it is a nearly limitless group of people who are motivated to share their knowledge and resources with anyone who wants to learn.

Disaster preparation isn't about spending thousands of dollars on the latest equipment and gear. While gear will help, you need to make sure you have the skills to use it. Having gear is great, but it shouldn't be the end-all answer.

Disaster preparedness isn't the easy way to success. Preparedness is just a mindset and lifestyle that allows you to start the process. Instead, it involves skills, knowledge, and resources gained over time. The more you put into disaster preparation, the better you chances of surviving when a big disaster does occur.

WHEN SHOULD YOU START?

Unfortunately, the best time to start preparing was about ten years or more ago. However, as the saying goes it's better late than never. Even if others are ahead of you when it comes to disaster preparation, this doesn't mean you can't start. Prepping can be done no matter how much spare time you have.

While truly mastering a skill is going to require more extensive time and knowledge; getting the basics can be done simply in the time it takes to read this book. Then after you finish this book, you will be able to break your preparation down into manageable chunks. Preparation isn't about keeping up with others; it's about knowing what your unique situation needs and getting prepared at your own pace.

Now let's take a moment to look at the layers of prepping so you can see how it is possible to break it down into manageable chunks.

You can choose to prepare for the worst-case scenario from the start, but as I said earlier, it's best to take things one step at a time to avoid mistakes. You should approach your disaster preparation as a set of layers.

LAYER 1: A 72-HOUR PLAN FOR BEGINNERS

The first step any person new to disaster preparedness needs to take is to learn the basics and be prepared to survive for at least 72 hours. Most small scale disaster won't last any longer than this, so it makes sense to have this plan in place first.

To complete this layer, you will need the following:

✓ A Bug Out Bag or BOB

✓ A first-aid kit

✓ A bug-out location and a designated safe room

✓ A bug-out vehicle

✓ A few basic survival skills and some specialized skills in an urban environment

✓ General physical preparation

✓ A few ways to start a fire

✓ A way to filter water

✓ Several light sources

✓ Multi-purpose survival items

- ✓ One thermal blanket per person

- ✓ A method of emergency communication

- ✓ Some form of self-defense

- ✓ A 72-hour stockpile of food based on 2,500 calories per day per person

- ✓ A three-day water stockpile based on one gallon per day per person

- ✓ Prepare mentally

- ✓ Know bug out routes

- ✓ Have a good, fixed-blade survival knife

- ✓ Have an understanding of COMSEC and OPSEC

RULE OF THREE

Keep in mind the survival rule of threes: you can live three minutes without air, three hours without shelter, three days without water and three weeks without food.

LAYER 2: THE THREE-WEEK PLAN

Obviously, once you have prepared the first layer, or 72-hour plan, you can expand it for the second layer, or three-week plan. It is best to ensure you have fully addressed layer one before moving on to layer two. However, there may always be some exceptions to every rule.

For layer two, you will need to add the following:

- ✓ Think about shelter if you are outside

- ✓ Know how to find water

- ✓ Learn how to start a fire without tools

- ✓ Expand your first aid kit

- ✓ Build a three-week water supply

- ✓ Build a three-week food supply

- ✓ Learn how to blend in with others

- ✓ Reorganize your home to find room for your new stockpile

- ✓ Fortify your home

- ✓ Make sure there's enough gas in your car to bug out

- ✓ Stock up on self-defense items and ammo if needed

- ✓ Have other means to transport supplies if your vehicle breaks down at some point

- ✓ Put together a get home bag or GHB, a car bug out bag and an everyday carry kit or EDC

- ✓ Have a fitness plan to stay in shape

LAYER 3: A THREE-MONTH EMERGENCY PLAN

At this point, you are preparing for a lot of bad things to happen. Since most people aren't prepared or able to survive past three weeks, you are also going to be facing dangerous individuals once you reach this level of survival. You are going to be up against well-prepared individuals with dwindling resources.

Depending on the nature of the disaster, this layer will require the following things:

✓ If you have a specific bug-out location, start stocking supplies there

✓ Develop a bug-out bag for your pets and make sure you have food stockpiled for them

✓ Develop plans for disaster scenarios likely to happen in your area and practice them

✓ Learn self-defense techniques

✓ Consider hiding locations for your supplies and gear

✓ Improve your health by focusing on changing your diet

✓ Have a means of cooking without electricity

✓ Develop a plan B and C for everything and stay flexible

LAYER 4: PREP FOR ONE YEAR OR MORE DISASTER

This layer, in my opinion, is more optional than required unless you really want to be ultimately prepared for everything that may happen.

If this is the case, you'll need to do the following:

- ✓ Stockpile seeds and learn gardening so you can have food for the long term

- ✓ Rotate your food stockpile at least twice a year and perhaps make it a part of your weekly diet

- ✓ Go off the grid

- ✓ Use alternate energy sources

- ✓ Collect rainwater

- ✓ Learn advanced skills like woodworking, plumbing, sewing, etc.

- ✓ Start raising backyard animals such as chickens, goats, ducks, pigs, cows, etc.

- ✓ Build a network of similar individuals as close to you as possible

- ✓ Learn bushcraft skills to survive adverse conditions

- ✓ Take survival classes

- ✓ Learn about renewable sources of food, water, and herbal medicine

- ✓ Get out of debt

- ✓ Consider moving to a location with a better survival context

- ✓ Start doubling up on important survival gear such as the following:

- Survival knife

- More means to start a fire

- Ways to purify water

- A second means of communication

✓ Learn a second language to make communication easier

✓ Get a 4x4 vehicle for easier bugging out in a disaster situation

✓ Learn to forage

✓ Modify your home or bug-out location

✓ Stockpile ways to have fun with no electronics or electricity

Now that you know all the layers of disaster preparation, the next step is to create a disaster plan. This is essential for knowing what you need to do to be prepared and how to get properly prepared.

CREATING A DISASTER PLAN

No matter where you live, your greatest risk of disaster comes from natural sources. Earthquakes, fires, floods, hurricanes, tornadoes, volcanic eruptions, blizzards, droughts, heat waves and even just severe storms have happened everywhere on the planet. Yet the majority of individuals don't have a plan in place for what to do in the event of a major natural disaster.

Either they think it won't happen to them, or they feel they can wait until the disaster is imminent and then let the government tell them what to do.

The reality is that having a disaster plan will help save your life, and it needs to be in place before an event occurs.

The first step in preparing for a disaster is to formulate a plan. You can't know what to buy for disaster preparedness without a plan to ensure you are spending your time and money wisely on the best equipment. Planning isn't that difficult and only requires a few steps.

The first step is to determine what types of disasters are likely to occur where you live. For example, those in the Midwest United States are going to need to do more preparation for tornadoes than those who live on the East Coast, where they may be more likely to experience hurricanes. Those who live in Japan do best to protect against typhoons and earthquakes.

When you know what disasters are more likely to happen in your area, you can plan better. Keep in mind that not only natural disasters but also human-made disasters can occur. Do you live near a chemical plant or a nuclear power plant?

Then you may want to prepare for chemical spills or a nuclear radiation threat. Are you in a region that often experiences cold winters? Then you should prepare for power failures and extreme cold. You should also consider what has historically worked in your area. All of these factors are important in developing a strong disaster preparedness plan.

Next, you need to identify a plan of action in the event of an emergency. The plan of action will include specific actions and steps to take when the disaster occurs. Some natural disasters, like hurricanes, have plenty of warning so you can decide what to do. Do you stay in your home or leave the area? Where will you go if you have to leave? Then there are disasters that occur unexpectedly, such as earthquakes.

Do you know if your area has emergency shelters? Do you know where to get disaster information? Are there relief agencies that will help you after such disasters?

The third step is to identify which supplies you will need after a natural disaster. Have an emergency survival kit together in advance, and make sure you have plenty of supplies on hand. The Federal Emergency Management Agency, or FEMA, recommends having enough to last seventy-two hours after a natural disaster, as we've shown in Layer One of disaster preparedness earlier.

When putting together a disaster plan with these three steps, there are a few factors to consider. Let's consider each of these individually.

The most important factor to consider is your location. What climate and terrain does your geography offer? If you live in a colder climate, you will need to pay extra attention to heat and shelter. You'll also have to consider snow and ice if you plan to bug out somewhere. Also, if you are far from your bug-out location, keep in mind that you may have to travel there on foot.

Another thing to consider is your family. A family with small children is going to require a different set of planning than, say, an elderly couple. The basic needs for food and hygiene are different, but there may also be additional needs, such as diapers or prescription medications. Another family member to consider is your pets and their specific needs. We'll discuss all of these special circumstances in the next chapter.

PERSONAL STRENGTHS AND WEAKNESSES

These are two important factors to consider when putting together a disaster preparedness plan. When you develop a plan that complements your strengths and reduces your weaknesses, you will be able to increase your chances of survival. If you are fit, you can carry more supplies and plan a longer escape route. If you know first aid, you can be a valuable member of a post-survival team.

Also, when you know your weaknesses, you will know which survival skills to train and learn. Do you know how to make a fire? Are you able to navigate? Do you know what plants are safe to eat in your area? All of these survival skills, and others, are very important for improving your chances of survival. Take the time to practice and learn to improve your strength. I will discuss the varied survival skills later.

PLAN A DESTINATION

It is recommended that, during survival planning, you identify at least four destinations. You should have one for each direction: North, South, East, and West. However, you can also add a fifth destination if you plan to bug in at your current home.

You can also narrow this option down if geography in your area makes traveling in a specific direction impossible. Having multiple bug-out locations and routes to each will improve the flexibility of your disaster preparedness plan. We'll talk more about choosing locations later.

Having a destination in mind is also important because it mentally improves your chances of survival. When you have a goal or a destination to reach, you can stay positive in your survival journey.

DETERMINE HOW FAST YOU CAN TRAVEL

This is also very important when planning your evacuation routes. If you know your average travel speed, you can calculate how many hours or days it will take you to reach your destination. This will affect the gear and supplies you will need to carry with you, or the skills you'll need to forage along the way. Your average travel speed will be determined by several factors.

WEIGHT OF YOUR PACK

The average person should carry no more than 25- 30 percent of their body weight. I am sure some of you can carry more, but it is strenuous and not feasible for long distances.

Therefore,, you will need to use this information to plan and pack your bug-out bag accordingly. It can even be a good idea to test your plan by carrying a bag with all your gear for a significant distance. Not only will you test your fitness ability to carry it, but you'll get a good idea of how fast you can travel while carrying your pack.

TERRAIN

The average walking speed for an individual with a weighted pack is 2.5 to 4 miles per hour on flat ground. However, your escape route should take into account what type of terrain you'll be covering. People often think that hiking downhill is faster than going uphill.

This is often untrue when it comes to hiking with a pack. When going downhill, you have to take extra care to avoid falling. Another thing to consider is whether you will need to cross a body of water or go through the rubble or mud. Plan a realistic pace to have the best plan outcome.

FITNESS

Obviously, a fit person can cover more ground at a faster rate than an unfit person. You need to realistically evaluate yourself in this situation. If you haven't hiked or gone for a run in awhile, then plan accordingly.

The best part of a disaster plan is that it brings out your weaknesses. This allows you to address any weak areas before they become an issue. If your disaster plan can benefit from additional exercise and fitness, then start planning now. We'll look at a good fitness plan in a later chapter.

OTHER MEMBERS OF YOUR GROUP

If you are planning to bug out in a group, then you are going to need to consider a few factors. If you have older adults or children in your group, they should be included in your preparedness planning so you know what resources and time you will need to assist them properly.

You can do this by planning your progress and routes based on how far and fast the least fit member of your group can travel.

ADDITIONAL FACTORS

Include a waterproof and/or laminated map in your bug-out gear, with your route and destination clearly marked. You may also want to include helpful landmarks along the route to improve your navigation.

If you are bugging out with a group, you should plan on setting a rallying point. When you do this in advance, you won't waste time trying to contact and locate each other after a major disaster when communications may be down or more difficult.

Have a list of emergency numbers for family, friends and government agencies. This way, you can stay in contact and up to date on what's going on around you.

While bugging out, plan to look for a place to sleep at least two to three hours before sunset. You might not like to lose this travel time, but it is better to shelter in place for the night rather than pushing it.

Your plan should include rest breaks and methods to keep yourself fueled and hydrated. The average 160-pound person burns about 400 calories per hour while hiking and nearly 500 calories per hour if they are carrying a full pack.

Once you've finished making a disaster preparedness plan, don't just put it somewhere. Rather, take the time to review it periodically to ensure it still meets your personal needs.

Creating a disaster plan is an important part of surviving a disaster. Following the above steps will help you create an effective plan that sets you on the road to proper disaster preparedness. Most of you reading this are probably new to disaster preparation, but since you read this far, I can safely assume you are in sync with me and serious about this topic. Let me give you some tips to help get started.

7 MUST-FOLLOW TIPS FOR NEW DISASTER PLANNERS

Most new disaster preparedness plans don't get started until a major event brings the idea to mind. In the world today, this seems to happen regularly. More and more people are taking the idea of disaster preparation seriously. If you're new to disaster preparation, you are taking the next step toward enjoying the benefits, as we've already discussed.

However, there is so much out there about disaster preparation, and it can be a little overwhelming for new preparers. This book is designed to take you back to basics and get you started on the right path. For this reason, I've listed seven tips below to help you get started on the right path when preparing for the first time.

1. WHAT SCENARIOS ARE YOUR PREPARING FOR?

The easiest and first tip for new preparers is to ask yourself what you are preparing for. You don't want to focus on everything at once, but you also don't want to put all your eggs in one basket. Each disaster requires a different preparation approach, but the basics tend to be the same.

2. FOCUS ON WATER AND FOOD

Once you start preparing, you will find a vast range of tools and gadgets available on the market. There are as many scams that promise you things as there are that do nothing more than take your money. Before you buy anything extra, focus on the two most important factors: water and food.

It is best to start with the 72-hour plan for water and food. However, eventually you should work up to a 30-day supply and improve your skills in sustainable food and water sources. Be sure to consider not only yourself but also your family and pets.

3. MAKE A LIST

When it comes to disaster preparedness, a list is very important. Make a list for each step of the preparation process. From the tools you need to the supplies in your first aid kit. Make a lot of lists. Consider keeping a notebook for your lists.

It is a good idea to have your lists written down rather than stored on a computer, since you will always have them with you in case the power goes down for an extended period. Even after you complete a list, you can keep it as a reference to know what you have.

4. LEARN NEW SKILLS

Once you have finished preparing your water and food, the next best thing you can do is focus on learning new skills. In an emergency or post-disaster situation, you may not be able to simply go to a grocery store to buy more food or take your car to the mechanic to get it fixed. When the SHTF, you need to be prepared to rely on your own skills to get by, and remember, you won't have the internet to look things up either.

5. KNOW HOW LONG YOU NEED TO PREPARE FOR

This goes along with knowing what you are preparing for. When you know how long you need to survive until help arrives or a situation improves, then you know what you need. For most natural disasters, you should aim to eventually have at least a week's worth of food, water, and supplies. From there, you can work your way up to any time frame you want, with the standard being thirty days. Some people will go as far as six or even twelve months.

6. KEEP IN MIND YOUR ENVIRONMENT

This is a useful tip for everyone, but it is especially important for those who live in regions of the globe where weather changes significantly across the seasons. If you start preparing in the summer, then make sure you also plan for the winter. Always plan for all seasons, no matter your current environment.

7. DON'T GET OVERWHELMED, STAY FOCUSED

This is possibly the best time for beginner preparers. It is easy to feel overwhelmed and scared when you first start out, given the events in the world and the amount of information available. The best way to get prepared is to stay focused and think about what you are trying to accomplish.

These seven tips will get you started on the right foot with disaster preparation. However, you can take your learning a step further by learning from others' mistakes. I've compiled a list of common disaster preparation mistakes for you to consider and to help you learn what not to do.

HOW TO AVOID 19 DISASTER PREPARATION MISTAKES

Preparing for a disaster and learning survival skills takes time to get right, so it's not uncommon for mistakes to happen. If you want to improve your disaster preparedness and survival skills, then consider some of the most common mistakes and learn from them.

NOT ENOUGH WATER

Surviving without food is possible for a month or so, but the body will start to shut down without water after just a couple of days. A common mistake is having plenty of food available, but no water. You should at least have a few gallons in your emergency kit, along with some filters and purification tablets.

You should also keep water on hand for cooking, washing, laundry and other tasks. While it won't have to be purified, you should still have it on hand.

NOT ENOUGH FOOD

Another common mistake is to keep only the bare minimum of non-perishable food on hand. Often, people simply want to feel prepared by having a few extra cans at home, but they don't actually make sure they have enough food for survival.

Along with this, you need to make sure you are prepared to use the food you stock. For example, if you store up grain, do you have a mill to process it? Know what is required to make food from your supplies and how to use them.

You also want to make sure you have a variety of foods stocked for a disaster. Remember to calculate how long you have to live off that food and make sure you are prepared to eat what you have for that long. Would you be able to eat the same food three times a day for months? Keep this in mind when choosing what to stockpile.

Depending on the situation you find yourself in, you can do fine with a stockpiled pantry for 48 hours to a week. However, don't ever think you can survive completely on store-bought food. Always have the skills needed to grow your own produce and possibly raise your own livestock so you can keep yourself well supplied in the longest of situations.

Even if you are well stocked with the right foods, it won't do you any good unless you rotate them. It is best to rotate your food every six months during daylight savings time to make things easier.

Perhaps the biggest food-and-water mistake people make is overestimating how long their supplies will last. So always try to double the amount of food and water you think you'll need on hand.

NO ALTERNATIVE COOKING METHOD

Freeze-dried food is great when the power goes out, but you should also have a few alternatives to warming and cooling food. Solar ovens, alcohol-fuel stoves, and outdoor fire cooking are just a few options you can learn.

FORGETTING VITAMINS AND MINERALS

Everyone focuses their survival stockpiles on high-calorie foods because they have macronutrients. However, most are forgetting their micronutrients. To survive, the body needs magnesium, zinc, vitamin C and other nutrients. Consider stocking up on multivitamins and mineral complexes as well.

RELYING ON TOO MUCH GEAR

It is always good to keep several flashlights and other assorted gadgets around the house. However, you should never rely solely on gear over the basics, such as food and water. It is important to focus on skills rather than gear. Gear won't do you any good if you don't know how to use it properly in a disaster.

NOT HAVING AN EVERYDAY CARRY KIT (EDC)

Disaster can strike at any time and place. If it happens when you are away from home, then an EDC can end up saving your life. It doesn't have to be anything large or fancy, but it does need to have the right supplies, and you need to know how to use them.

BEING TOO CHEAP

While the point is to try to be prepared while spending as little as possible, you also need to keep in mind that you get what you pay for. For example, getting a cheap survival knife could have fatal consequences. We'll discuss more about how to save money at the end of this book, but for now, I'll advise you to know where to cut corners and when to spend more for a good-quality product.

NOT PLANNING FOR SELF-DEFENSE

Even when a minor disaster or event occurs, people start taking the law into their own hands. During a major event, there may not even be a law to rely on for assistance. Therefore, you need to plan some form of self-defense. This doesn't mean you have to carry a weapon if you are uncomfortable with this option.

In fact, you don't want to rely on firearms. However, you can learn non-lethal forms of self-defense such as batons, stun guns, pepper spray or tactical pens. Find a self-defense option that suits you, and you become confident in its use.

NOT HAVING AN ALTERNATIVE PLAN

Most people assume they will be at home during a disaster and keep all their gear there. What would you do if a disaster were to strike when you were at work or not at home? It is a good idea to have a plan to get you back home, along with a mini get-home bag with extra survival gear.

THINKING YOU'LL NEVER HAVE TO LEAVE HOME

For a short-term emergency, you can probably survive at home. Depending on your surroundings, it is obviously a safe option. However, if the situation changes, you may have to leave your home. Also, if you live in the city, it could become a death trap in a post-disaster situation, and you will need to move out. So, make sure you have a backup plan if you need to leave your home.

NOT PROPERLY SECURING YOUR HOME

If you feel you should bug in rather than bug out after a disaster, make sure your home is as secure as possible. Intruders will be persistent after a disaster, and there may be no law enforcement around to help. We'll discuss later the specifics on how you can fortify your home to protect yourself after a disaster.

NOT HAVING A BUG OUT LOCATION AND ESCAPE ROUTE

If your home is no longer safe, you need to have a bug-out location in mind. Later in this book, we will discuss how you can choose the best bug-out location. However, once you have chosen a location, you will also need to plan an escape route in advance.

This requires you to know your area well. You should have at least three different escape routes mapped and planned out as part of your disaster preparedness.

NEGLECTING BASIC SKILLS

I've said it before, and I'll say it again: you need to focus on your skills. All the stockpiled water, food and supplies will do you no good if you don't have skills. The skills you know are what are really going to matter when SHTF.

NOT BEING IN SHAPE

While this isn't exactly true in all situations, after all, there are disabled and elderly people who can survive after a disaster; you certainly want to do what you can to improve your physical fitness. Make sure you have the strength, stamina, and endurance needed to survive.

NOT HAVING A BACKUP PLAN

No one knows exactly how a disaster will unfold or how society will be reshaped after a major event. Therefore, you always need several backup plans for your main survival plan. There are a number of things that can go wrong or change when it comes to survival; for this, you need multiple backup plans in place.

NOT DOING ENOUGH RESEARCH

This can be true in a number of ways. Have you researched the place where you live to determine all of the hidden dangers? Perhaps your area hasn't had an earthquake in over 10 years, but does it sit on a major fault line? You should always thoroughly research your area to ensure you are prepared for everything likely to happen there.

This can also apply to your prepping when it comes to gear. Have you truly researched all aspects of the gear to make sure you are getting the best? Have you done all the research needed to make sure you know how to use it? Knowledge and skills are two things you can never have enough of, and you gain knowledge by doing your research.

NOT MAINTAINING AND ORGANIZING INVENTORY

Don't be one of those individuals who buy supplies, store them and then forget about them until they really need them. It is important to keep an inventory of items on hand and know where they are at all times. You should also check your inventory regularly to maintain and change it if something in your living situation changes. You also want to make sure you know how to use everything that you have stocked and keep practicing your skills, so you don't forget what to do when the time comes.

NOT PRACTICING

Skills are the key to survival; planning is the key to knowing which skills you need. However, none of this will work if you don't practice regularly and know exactly what you need to do. If you don't do something regularly, then you are sure to forget it.

FORGETTING THE BARTER VALUE

Just because you don't have a use for something doesn't mean someone else won't. Always keep in mind that bartering will become mainstream after a major event. Therefore, consider something carefully before assuming it is useless and discarding it.

There are many situations in life where you can learn from your mistakes, but you won't be able to do this in a post-disaster situation. When the SHTF, you won't be able to get a second chance, and you'll need to do everything to the best of your ability the very first time.

Learn from these mistakes now so you can be better prepared for the future. Now let's look at some special considerations that might make disaster preparation a little more challenging for you.

SPECIAL PREPPING CONSIDERATIONS

GETTING YOUR LOVED ONES TO PREPARE

One would think that, with all the work involved, there are many difficulties in disaster preparation. However, the greatest difficulty by far is the fact that your friends and family, in particular, are oblivious to your idea of prepping and its importance.

Getting other members of your family to prepare isn't easy, and if it is a friend, you probably wouldn't bother. However, when it comes to loved ones, you want to protect them and feel they should get prepared along with you. So how can you get your family on board with your disaster preparation plans if they don't want to?

SHOULD YOU FORGET EVERYONE ELSE?

Should you just forget anyone who doesn't share your mindset? If you don't see someone often enough to influence them, do you waste your time trying to get them to prepare? For most people, even if they see the same information and facts you've seen, such as those at the start of this book, they may not come to the same logical conclusions as you did. Otherwise, they would be right there with you in your disaster preparation.

People basically start preparing for a disaster for one of two reasons: desperation and inspiration.

An example of desperation is an individual who doesn't prepare until they see imminent danger, such as a hurricane warning. Others will see the desperation after they've actually survived a disaster. At this point, they realize that not preparing is the most dangerous thing of all.

On the other hand, inspiration is individuals who are exposed to information, connect the dots and make sense of the world around them. They realize how dangerous the world is becoming and feel the need to prepare, even if something isn't likely to happen in their area.

If you want to change someone from a state of desperation to an inspirational mindset, you need to be close to them. The people who live in the same house as you, who spend a lot of time with you or even those who share your hobbies and passions.

This is because these individuals trust you and often share your concerns. It is more challenging with an individual at work, a neighbor or any other individual you may not see that often.

WHY GET YOUR FAMILY TO PREPARE?

The simple answer is that you won't be able to prepare unless your family is doing it with you. You and your family are in the same position; you live in the same house or, at the very least, live in the same location that will be affected by the disaster. During a disaster, you won't be able to leave your family behind, no matter how unprepared they are.

Rather, you'll do your best to help them. When SHTF, your family will act just like the rest of the public. They won't know what to do, or they'll just try to hide out until it all goes away and returns to normal. This could negatively affect you as well.

It is difficult to convince someone who's not ready to put money and effort into something that may never happen, but when it comes to your family, you should try. You love your family, and you can influence them.

You can get your family on board, but only if you approach them the right way. When approaching family, most people do it the wrong way, which leads to failure. Most feel the best way is to scare people with apocalyptic scenarios that are really difficult to grasp or imagine. Therefore, you get nowhere. This is how the human mind works.

Think about yourself and how you got into the mindset to prepare. You have to learn information, let it sink in, do some additional research and then maybe talk to someone about disaster preparation before you even get started. You had to wait for the dots to appear before you could connect them. You need to use the same mindset when trying to get your family on board.

START SMALL

If you want to get your loved ones on board, you need to start small. Focus on small-scale events at first; those that can happen close to home or are already happening in your area. Talk to your family about these events, but don't scare them or rush them to prepare. Rather, just talk and show them the dots and allow them to connect. Keep things believable, so they can realize the importance of being prepared.

Once you have your family on board, you can all start prepping together. But what if you have an elderly or disabled family member? Or what if you have a disability that makes it difficult to bug out in an emergency? If either of these is true for you, keep reading about disaster preparation for disabled people.

PREPPING FOR THE DISABILITIES

Do a search online, and you can find plenty of information on preparing and bugging out during an emergency. However, most of this information is geared towards those who are fit and able. There is little to no information on what to do if you or someone you love isn't in the best of health or is physically disabled. How can you ensure all members of your family can survive, regardless of their health status?

As with regular disaster preparation, the key is to consider potential problems before they occur. Knowledge and proper planning can go a long way to successfully evacuating all family members in an emergency. Think about plausible future scenarios and how they will impact your survival plans.

When planning for disasters with disabled individuals, there are many additional things you need to consider and keep in mind, including the following:

✧ Medications

✧ Medical equipment

✧ Mobility devices

✧ Mode of transportation

✧ Service animals

Let's look at how you can modify your plan to accommodate people with disabilities. Keep in mind that when I refer to disabled individuals, I'm including anyone who is less-abled, not just disabled physically or elderly individuals. The ultimate goal is to ensure that all loved ones have what they need to survive an emergency while remaining as comfortable as possible.

3 SPECIAL CONSIDERATIONS

First of all, let's consider the special considerations you need to take into account when preparing for a disaster with anyone who is disabled. In addition, while preparing, you will need to stockpile additional supplies and have additional maintenance knowledge of other equipment.

MEDICATIONS

This section can include any number of people, even those who aren't disabled. Many people are taking prescription medications, and you need to keep this in mind when preparing for a disaster. It is important that you talk with your doctor first before you start stockpiling any prescription medications.

The first step is to make a list of all required medications, the doses and when/how often you take them. Have this list, along with copies of your prescriptions, in your BOB just in case you need the information. Pharmacies often only stock three days' worth of medication and are usually the first target for looters. This means it is best to plan ahead for events that may disrupt your medicine supply.

Ideally, you want to have 90 to 180 days' worth of medications on hand. This will be enough to get you through most events, and particularly if you have a good relationship with your doctor, discuss having some extra supply of medications and be honest with them.

There are some legal options for getting extra medications to store beyond your initial supply. If your condition allows for it (ask your doctor); you can skip doses by taking every other one, cutting doses in half or even skipping one dose a week to develop your stockpile. If you plan a trip similar to bug out, ask your doctor or a travel clinic in your area for extra refills to cover you.

For those traveling overseas, you can often see a doctor on your visit and then fill a prescription that you bring back with you. Customs will typically allow a three-month supply as long as it is in the original packaging, accompanied by the prescription, and it is for personal use for a serious condition.

In addition to stockpiling prescription medications, you should also search for natural alternatives. There are homeopathic medicines, natural treatments and herbal remedies for a variety of conditions. When all other options run out, this may be your last choice. Plus, they are perfectly legal to stockpile.

EQUIPMENT

There are several types of equipment to consider for disabled individuals.

First, let's consider mobility equipment. You should maintain the equipment to ensure it is always in proper working order. Should electricity fail, you should have a way to keep batteries charged. A solar charger is often your best option. Make sure you have a higher-wattage charger or solar panel so you can fully charge these batteries.

You may also want to consider having a backup mobility device, such as extra canes, walkers or wheelchairs. It is best to have a non-electric backup, such as a folding wheelchair. This is especially important if you plan to bug out during an emergency and your vehicle can't accommodate a large mobility device.

If possible, you should have the spare equipment stored in a separate outbuilding. This way, if the primary equipment is damaged, it won't affect the spare equipment.

If you need to replace an older piece of equipment, keep the old one as a backup as long as it still functions properly and doesn't pose a safety risk. Even if the old equipment doesn't fit as well or isn't as comfortable as the newer option, it will get you by when you can't readily replace it.

If you haven't already, make sure your home has ramps and pathways that make it easier to get around both inside and outside.

If you need equipment such as oxygen tanks or other breathing apparatus, then talk with your doctor about having an extra supply on hand. You may not be able to have several months' worth stocked up, but even a month or two of extra supplies might last you during a disaster.

TRANSPORTATION

If you plan to bug out during an emergency or think you might need to transport a disabled person, you should have a vehicle that can meet those needs. If you can't transport the disabled individual, you'll need to bug in at your current location.

Most people can manage in a regular car or truck, but people with severe disabilities will need a special van or bus to travel. Have a plan established to make sure all bases are covered.

When traveling with disabled individuals, you don't want to wait until the last minute. It is best to move to a safe location early on, rather than being stuck in traffic with everyone else trying to evacuate.

When making a plan to bug out, you should always account for potential kinks. Consider the following questions when planning for all possible scenarios:

✧ Can you bug out with a vehicle?

✧ Will you be traveling on foot?

✧ Can you redistribute the weight of your BOB?

✧ Does the disabled person have any mobility?

✧ Could you carry the disabled person if needed?

✧ Can the disabled person handle the stress of bugging out?

Plan for all possible scenarios, test your plan, alter if necessary and then test again. Repeat the process until you have the best possible plan down and know exactly what you are doing.

THREE SCENARIOS

When preparing for disabilities, there are three scenarios to consider.

1. Bugging in at your location.

2. Planning to bug out with a disabled person.

3. Making your own disaster plan if you have limitations.

BUGGING IN AT YOUR LOCATION

Most prepares are ready to bug in during less severe events, but they are also prepared to bug out if there is a major event or if things get really serious. Unfortunately, if you or a loved one is disabled, this may not be an option. The option to buy out will depend on how severely disabled a person is, the level of preparedness you have done and the type of transportation you have access to.

If you can meet the requirements of bugging out to a different location and have a way to get there, even with a disability, then you have a distinct advantage over others. However, if you aren't able to bug out, then your next best option is to have a bug-in setup ready at your home.

When you have a stock of medications, equipment, and necessary supplies, you can continue to live with some level of comfort while tending to other necessities such as security, food, water and keeping warm and comfortable.

Another option is to have a plan in place to get a disabled person to a hospital with generators. This way, life-saving equipment can continue to run.

PLANNING TO BUG OUT WITH A DISABLED PERSON

The first step is to ensure you realistically evaluate the disabled person's ability to move long distances. Know how much movement they can do. Are they able to walk a full day or less?

Some people will need your help to be mobile, while others can improve their mobility with aids like walking sticks. If limitations can be overcome through fitness or lifestyle changes, be sure to encourage your family to start making them now.

If you plan to bug out with disabled individuals, then make a plan to accommodate their needs. If possible,, use a car or other vehicle to cover some ground and plan to drive as far as you can before heading out on foot. If you are planning on using a car in your bug-out plan, then you should consider the following:

Make sure you have the right vehicle, a vehicle bug-out kit, and your own BOB.

Have alternate locations in your bug-out plan in case you can't reach your car or need to travel in a different direction from the one you originally planned.

Packing for a person with disabilities can be difficult since they may only be able to carry a light BOB or none at all. If you are traveling in a group, distribute the disabled person's gear evenly among the other members so you don't burden one person more than the others and can maximize the group's ability to travel.

Make sure your BOB includes items that make camp as comfortable as possible. The more comfortable a person is, the better they can recover and travel further the next day. Consider things like a larger bed roll or a lightweight folding stool for rest breaks.

Even if a person has fair mobility and can travel a decent distance, you should still plan to ease the hard impact of travel. A bug-out vehicle is still important in these situations. If you have to travel on foot, make sure the disabled individual doesn't have as much of a burden as others.

MAKING YOUR OWN DISASTER PLAN IF YOU HAVE LIMITATIONS

Let's move to the last scenario, in which you are the one with a physical limitation, meaning you need an adapted bug-out plan. If you have family members who will help you, share the tips above with them to make sure everyone is prepared in case you need to bug out in an emergency.

However, if you don't have anyone to help you, then you should develop a bug-out plan that meets your individual needs.

The first step in developing a modified plan is to perform a realistic assessment of your abilities. After this, you can determine whether to bug in, as in the first step, or bug out and follow the steps in the second segment.

CONSIDER CAREGIVERS

Most disabled individuals will have family or friends they can rely on when something happens. However, there are times when the disabled person is alone or using a caregiver. This can be a difficult situation, but there are still some things you can do. Consider asking your caregiver to help with the following:

Ask them to buy a few extra groceries when they shop for you, this way you can gradually build your stockpile of food and water.

Ask them to help you plant a small garden or grow vegetables in pots.

Ask them to help make the necessary changes to your home environment so it will be easier for you to bug out on your own during a disaster.

You should also try to build a community of people who can help you in an emergency. If you don't have family or friends close by, consider asking neighbors, coworkers or others in your life who are willing to help you.

CONSIDER SERVICE ANIMALS

If you or a loved one has a service animal, you also need to plan to care for their well-being. It's about the same as preparing for a pet, as I will discuss that soon. The only exception is that a service animal is much more important for your safety and survival.

Make sure you have water, food, and medications stocked up for your service animal. If the service animal is a dog, then have some extra collars and leashes on hand as well. A service animal is likely already well-trained, but you can do additional training to make sure your service animal knows what to do in emergency situations, such as the following:

✧ Providing protection

✧ Being desensitized to strange noises and smells

✧ Providing additional services like pulling a cart or carrying a pack

If you have a disability, you have likely already made changes to your home. If you haven't, you should work to get these in place before a disaster happens. Otherwise, you can focus on planning and preparing for bugging out in the event of a disaster.

PREPPING WITH CHILDREN

Even on a good day, it can be difficult to raise children. Anyone who has raised or is currently raising a family knows this all too well. Being entrusted with life is a huge responsibility.

It is made even harder if you are a single parent and need to rely on others for assistance. Now, combine all of these difficulties with the need to prepare and know what to do in the event of a major disaster.

When it comes to family disaster preparedness, teaching your children the basics is essential. Children are generally curious, and with careful nurturing, you can teach them the skills needed to save their lives in a disaster.

You really can start at any age to teach your children to be prepared. For example, you can simply turn a game of hide and seek into a valuable learning game. If you are doing it outdoors, you can teach them to use the surrounding environment for camouflage and shelter.

As a child gets older, they can move on to more challenging subjects. You can teach them about fishing, so they know how to sustain their food sources. It is also a good idea to teach them about gun safety and use at some point.

Also, it can be helpful to teach self-defense or martial arts skills because it not only equips them with valuable self-defense skills but also instills discipline, respect, confidence, and perseverance.

You should teach your child to swim as soon as possible. In fact, there are plenty of things you can teach a child about bushcraft skills from an early age, including knots, weaving, water filtration and more.

When you give your children a solid start with basic preparedness skills, you are giving them a good foundation. The children can then build on it and pass it along to their children. Ensuring that all future generations are ready in the event of a major disaster.

PET PREPPING

Preparing yourself for an emergency is one thing, but what about your four-legged family members? Your pets depend on you for everything, and unlike human family members, they can't learn survival skills to help keep them safe in an emergency.

Disaster preparation with your pets is just like preparing with people, but with just a few differences. With careful planning and attention to a few details, you will be able to survive any disaster with your pets.

Take the time to think of what you would do if you could never go to the pet store again. What would you need to do to transition your pet to an off-the-grid lifestyle? This is the best question to start with to help you successfully prep for your pet.

WHAT TO PREP

When SHTF, pets require the same basic items we do. You can start with a broad list and then tailor it to your pets' specific needs to make sure they are taken care of.

WATER AND FOOD

If an emergency turns into a long-term survival situation, then you are going to need to find a more abundant source of pet food than the pet store. For a small-scale disaster, having a backup supply of food for your pet should be enough.

The same applies to water. Dogs can drink water from pretty much anywhere, but cats and other animals might be more discerning. You should have a good idea of how much water your animals drink each day. Make sure you have enough safe drinking water on hand to allow them to make it through a major emergency.

Ideally, you should stock at least three days' worth of food and water per animal. The best is to have a week's worth. If you have to transition your pet to food they don't normally eat, plan for a few days to get them used to it.

MEDICATION

If your pet takes medication daily or monthly, you should keep a backup of this on hand, just as you would for humans. Also, keep in mind the backups of flea collars, heartworm medicine, and animal-specific medications. At least an extra month of any medication, plus a year's worth of heartworm medication, is recommended.

FIRST AID

You should also have a first-aid kit specifically designed for your pets on hand. Animals can get hurt just like humans, but their different size means that a standard human first aid kit likely won't work for them.

The best way to know what to include in an animal's first-aid kit is to talk to your veterinarian. They know what is best for your specific pet and can help you make the best decisions. However, the basics still apply when it comes to the following:

✦ Isopropyl alcohol

✦ Gauze bandages

✦ Cotton bandage rolls

- ✧ Antibiotic ointment

- ✧ Scissors

- ✧ Saline solution

CARRIER, COLLAR, AND LEASH

Cats and dogs typically wear collars at all times. However, if this isn't the case, then you should have one on hand for when the SHTF. The same applies to a leash and a carrier. Even if you don't typically use a leash or carrier, you should have them on hand in case of an emergency.

Having a carrier on hand is crucial in getting your pet evacuated in a hurry. Some animals will freak out in an emergency, making them difficult to handle. When you place your pet in a carrier, you can keep them calm and safe while also saving time when moving them to another location.

EVERYTHING ELSE

Indoor animals often need some form of bedding for waste needs. For a cat, this is often the kitty litter, and for smaller pocket pets, it is some kind of wood chips. No matter what your pet uses, you should have a backup of it to help ease your pet into the new situation.

PUTTING A PLAN TOGETHER

Even after you have the necessary supplies on hand, you still need to have a plan to handle your pets in an emergency. You will have a plan for yourself and your family, so you'll definitely want one for your pets.

Have someone in your family responsible for each animal, and make sure everyone knows where the emergency supplies and carriers are located. Know how you'll fit the supplies and carriers into your car or truck along with your other emergency supplies. Practice moving your animals on occasion so there aren't any surprises when the real thing happens.

Being organized and prepared is the key to surviving with your pets. If you have a pet, they aren't just living in your house; they are a part of the family. Include them in your prepping and don't leave them behind.

PREPARING YOURSELF FOR A DISASTER

Everyone can learn to prepare themselves and become self-sufficient in the event of a disaster; all it takes is some time, effort and energy. Think for a moment what would happen if you didn't have any modern conveniences or luxuries; what would you do? Do you have the skills needed to meet your basic needs? Would you be physically fit enough to survive a long-term disaster scenario? If you're not sure about the questions above, keep reading. In this chapter, we are going to discuss how you can prepare yourself to become more self-sufficient and get prepared for any disaster.

5 MUST-HAVE SKILLS TO LEARN

Thanks to modern conveniences, most of us don't need to learn all the little skills we used to need to live our daily lives. However, this doesn't mean you should never learn these skills. While these skills may seem time-consuming and labor-intensive to learn, they can be the difference between life and death in a survival situation.

For example, when was the last time you needed to start a fire with flint and steel to cook your dinner? Probably never, but would this save your life in an emergency? Definitely. So, let's consider the skills you should learn to be prepared for a disaster

FIXING AND REPAIRING

Consumer goods have made things readily available, so most simply throw away something when it no longer functions as intended, rather than repairing. When you know how to repair everyday items, you are increasing your self-sufficiency while also saving money and resources.

To start, go online and watch DIY videos to learn how to fix common items around your home. You should also take the time to study the items to understand how they work, so you can easily identify what's wrong when something doesn't. You should also stock up on the common supplies and tools you will need to fix and repair things.

GARDENING

This can be a bit difficult to practice if you don't have much land to cultivate. However, there are ways to learn and develop basic gardening skills with even the smallest of areas. Gardening is valuable in providing you with a sustainable food source after a disaster hits.

If you happen to live in an apartment or a condo, you can try container gardening. Look it up on Google or watch a YouTube video to see how it is done. You may be surprised how container gardening can be a good source of food supply for your family. My wife is an avid container gardener; she grows all her herbs in containers right on our back porch.

COOKING

Cooking from scratch is also important, since you won't have processed or pre-cooked foods in an emergency. Think of the foods you'll be stockpiling; most are ingredients and not ready-to-eat food. In addition to practicing cooking from scratch, you also want to learn multiple cooking methods and fire-building skills, so you will always have a way to prepare your food.

FIRST AID

Getting CPR certification is also a way to become self-sufficient. When you know what to do in an emergency, it helps you stay calm and successful when SHTF. American and other Red Cross facilities around the world offer free CPR courses that you can take and be certified in just a few hours. Here is a link to the American Red Cross CPR training course.

http://www.redcross.org/take-a-class/cpr

REPURPOSING

This is the ability to turn items you have into things you need. When you can find alternative uses for items, it will be very valuable for survival situations. Just a few examples include making fishhooks from animal bones, using garbage bags as windbreakers, cooking from scraps and making a bow from skis.

I am sure you get the idea. Just open the creative side of your brain, look at any object and come up with at least 5 different uses for that object. See if you can, try it now.

11 TYPES OF SURVIVAL SKILLS YOU SHOULD MASTER

The list of skills you can learn to survive is quite extensive. In fact, there is too much for me to go into detail in this book. So, I'm just going to provide you with a list of survival skills. That way, you have an idea of what you can learn.

If something interests you, simply research, learn and then practice that skill till you master it. I call it the "rinse and repeat" process. Pick a few from the list that interest you, then start the process. In a few weeks, you will be able to master more than you can imagine.

FOOD, WATER, COOKING, AND HOMESTEADING SKILLS

Finding water

Purifying water

Baking bread

Baking without powder

Growing and drying herbs

Dehydrating foods

Smoking foods

Pasteurizing milk

Gardening skills

Making cheese

Composting

Harvesting seeds

Freeze-drying foods

Canning foods

Cooking on a fire

HUNTING AND FISHING SKILLS

Making snares

Reading animal tracks

Fishing using a variety of methods

Shooting a slingshot

FIRST AID AND MEDICAL SKILLS

Giving first aid

Performing CPR

Carrying a wounded person

Treating sunstroke, hypothermia, and dehydration

Treating open wounds

Treating scrapes for infections

Splinting a broken limb

Recognizing and using wild medicinal plants

Treating bullet wounds

Treating knife wounds

Treating bite wounds

Epidemiology

Suturing

ON THE MOVE SKILLS

Navigation

Reading a topographic map

Staying hidden

Bugging out

Getting out of a riot

Getting out of a city

Escaping buildings

Dealing with mobs and protesters

Escape and evasion

Driving

SELF-DEFENSE SKILLS

Shooting a weapon

Basic self-defense moves

Cleaning a gun

Zeroing a gun

Making basic weapons

MENTAL SKILLS

Stress management

Reading people

Conserving your energy

Leadership

Managing boredom and loneliness

Motivating people

Goal setting

Self-reliance

Becoming a gray man

COMMUNICATION SKILLS

Using a HAM radio

Using non-conventional writing methods

Bartering

INTERMEDIATE SURVIVAL SKILLS

Splitting Firewood

Tying a bowline knot

Climbing a tree

Making mosquito traps and repellents

Milking a cow or goat

Cutting a tree

Washing clothes

Making homemade laundry soap or detergent

Navigating without GPS

Sharpening cutting tools

Building a long-term shelter

Opening cans and bottles without an opener

Grooming without modern products or conveniences

Identifying edible plants

Sewing, knitting, quilting and crocheting

Telling time

WOODWORKING SKILLS

Building a beehive

Making a greenhouse

Making a chicken brooder

Building a fence

How to use a saw and a chainsaw

Making a chicken coop

Building an aquaponics system

Constructing a meat smokehouse

ADVANCE SURVIVAL SKILLS

Making improvised rope

Making a rope bridge

Mechanical aptitudes

Escaping Quicksand

Butchering an animal

Gutting an animal

Plumbing

Welding

Electrical skills

Construction skills

Assisting a birth

Working with metal

Working with clay

Digging a well

Building boats and rafts

Brick making

Plucking a chicken

Making paper

Meteorology

Making candles

Making an oil lamp

Making a solar lamp

Grinding wheat

OTHER SKILLS

Horseback riding

Tanning hides

Fixing clothes

Making bags and baskets

Making homemade beauty products

Learning a second language

Learning new skills is just a part of preparing for a disaster. You should also focus on dropping addictive or harmful habits. Let's look at how to do this and why it can benefit your disaster preparation.

DROPPING BAD HABITS

There are four main bad habits that impede many individuals' ability to become self-sufficient and, as a result, make it harder for them to prepare for disasters. These are addictions, poor diet, low activity level and a negative attitude.

ADDICTIONS

The dependence of a chemical substance limits your self-sufficiency and chances of survival because it can cloud your thinking and have a negative effect on your health. If you're a smoker, try to quit smoking using a method that works for you. While E-cigs have become popular among those trying to quit, they still contain nicotine and should be avoided.

If you have an addiction to drugs or alcohol, consider finding a local AA group that can help you get over your addiction. Dependence on alcohol or drugs will affect your emotional and physical health, making it more difficult to deal with intense situations.

I used to be a heavy smoker, and when I couldn't smoke, I became irritated very easily, had a hard time concentrating and often felt depressed. Now think about it, if I were in a disaster situation and could not find a cigarette to smoke, would I be able to concentrate and focus to do what I need to do to survive?

If you happen to rely on my support for survival, would I be a good support? Knowing what I know now, I wouldn't rely on my old self. So free yourself from all addiction. I know it is hard at first, but I did it, and I know you can too.

POOR DIET

Your body is like a machine, and what you put in it is the fuel that determines its performance. When you overeat or have poor nutrition, it can limit your potential and negatively impact your overall health and well-being.

Look for foods that pack nutrients and learn to cook meals you'll enjoy. When shopping for groceries, try to examine the nutrition labels closely to make sure you are getting the best possible foods for your body.

I do know it is hard to eat healthy every day or every meal, as life as we know it is getting busier by the day. So do what I do: I have started juicing 3x a week so I can get all the nutrients I might be missing from other foods throughout the week. Juicing is a great way to be healthy. If you haven't seen the documentary "Fat, Sick, and Nearly Dead," by all means watch it; it can be an eye-opening experience. This documentary motivated me to start juicing.

LOW ACTIVITY LEVEL

There are many temptations in today's society. Most of these temptations are designed to encourage a sedentary life. While it is impossible to completely banish technology these days, you should try to balance both downtime and activity.

Self-sufficiency requires strength and endurance. Once you achieve these goals, you need to maintain them. It is best to start with low-impact activities for beginners and then gradually work up to more advanced training.

NEGATIVE ATTITUDE

Often, the greatest difficulty to overcome is your own thoughts and beliefs. When you find yourself in a survival situation, a negative attitude will impact your ability to think on your feet and make good decisions. To improve your attitude, you should adopt an optimistic, positive approach to situations and express gratitude regularly.

The thought of becoming self-sufficient can be difficult with all the conveniences and luxuries today. However, if you start gradually, you can improve your life and make yourself more self-sufficient. Lastly, I want you to consider the role of fitness in disaster preparedness and ways to improve your physical health.

DISASTER PREPARATION AND FITNESS

In an emergency, there are a number of things you may have to do that require physical fitness. In addition, we are talking about possibly living in a world without computers, cars or other modern-day conveniences. As a result, survival fitness doesn't mean perfecting your body to meet fitness model standards; rather, it means conditioning your body to a level that allows it to handle the physical tasks necessary after a disaster. This is why fitness is an important part of your disaster preparedness plan.

You can stockpile all the supplies you want and learn all the skills you can, but it won't do you much good if you physically can't survive the environment around you. You need to start conditioning your body to sustain the physical toll it will undergo when surviving off the grid.

Fitness preparation isn't about aesthetics or running an extra mile; rather, it is about gradually increasing your body's ability to handle tasks related to your survival when a disaster takes out all the modern conveniences. Starting a survival fitness routine is something you can start today and see benefits later. Physical fitness will help augment any number of your survival skills.

To maximize your survival fitness, you need to consider your bug-out plan and consider all the activities you may need to perform to follow it. We are going to look at some common scenarios likely to arise in a disaster situation and provide workout ideas to help you achieve your fitness goals.

However, keep in mind that you may need to talk to your doctor first to make sure you are in good enough health and able to start a fitness routine safely.

THE FOUR PRINCIPLES OF SURVIVAL FITNESS

If you want to be physically fit and prepared for a disaster, then there are four principles or areas you need to focus on with survival fitness.

1. Strength

2. Stamina

3. Flexibility

4. Speed

Even if you can only improve on each of these four areas a little bit each week, you are going to greatly increase your chances of survival. But think of how these things can benefit you. Strength is needed to lift heavy objects or people and possibly fight off attackers.

Stamina is important because you don't want to run out of breath after hiking for ten minutes with a pack. Flexibility is important if you are trying to run, jump, climb or do any other type of activity. Lastly, speed is important when you have to run for your life.

If you read about my earlier life, then you know at age 27 I was diagnosed with high blood pressure, borderline diabetes, obesity and being overweight. I could not even walk 100 yards. Since then till now, I have changed my life completely, and you know I have been hiking for many years now and have hiked in over 17 countries,

I shared some of my hiking experience and knowledge in my first book, "Complete Hiking & Backpacking Guide." The point I am making is that if you can just take up walking or take mini hiking trips, it can totally change your life and prepare you for anything that comes your way.

SEVEN EFFECTIVE WAYS TO IMPROVE YOUR FITNESS LEVEL

WALKING

Walking is the easiest and healthiest way to start conditioning your body for endurance, and it is something the whole family can get involved in doing. Walking will build your physical endurance and condition you to walk several miles, which can be essential for reaching your bug-out location.

The American Heart Association recommends at least 150 minutes of moderate-intensity aerobic exercise per week when you first start. As your strength increases, you can cover more distance and handle more difficulty with rougher terrain and steeper inclines.

CARRY WEIGHT

After you've conditioned yourself with walking, the next milestone you can set is to walk the same distance while carrying the weight of your BOB or other necessities you'll be carrying during a crisis. However, you don't want to exhaust yourself right away, so you should start slow by carrying your bag only partially full for the first couple of weeks.

Work your way up to carrying a full pack the full distance to your bug-out location. This is also a great exercise to identify any non-essential, heavy items you can remove from your BOB. You can also make a fun camping trip out of it with your family, gradually increasing the difficulty of the trail that leads to your campsite.

GO FOR A RUN

While a bug-out scenario should only require walking, there are sometimes when you may need to increase your pace or possibly run for your life. You should start early in your fitness training to condition your body for bursts of speed that gradually increase in duration.

Sprint training can easily be added to your walking routine by doing a vigorous sprint every five to ten minutes. Sprints are the best way to increase your heart rate and condition your body. However, sprints will also add strain to your joints and muscles. So, you should stretch well before and after doing this type of exercise routine.

You can eventually step up your walk-sprints to a jog, then a full-on run. You only need to run for 75 minutes a week to gain cardiovascular health benefits, including weight loss.

STRENGTH

Cardio training is important for getting you to your bug-out location, but strength training is necessary to help you overcome obstacles you may encounter along the way. The general increase in activity can also help you when living off the grid. The level of strength needed depends on your individual situation, location, and bug-out crew.

To build your core, you don't need a lot of equipment or a gym membership. There are plenty of home exercises you can do to improve your core. You can do push-ups, sit-ups, and squats using your own body weight for resistance. Or you can take up a sport to build your fitness routine.

Any level will work to start, and there are plenty of options for playing sports both indoors and outdoors, so you have year-round access. For the adventurous sort, rock climbing is an excellent sport that provides a full-body workout. I will admit I am not good at rock climbing, but it is a great way to build endurance and stamina, for sure.

FLEXIBILITY

When improving your physical fitness, you should never forget flexibility. Flexible joints are important for preventing discomfort and injury while performing the tasks that bug out requires. Building flexibility can be done by simply adding stretches to your fitness routine or doing a flexibility-oriented activity like yoga.

WATER EXERCISES

For the purpose of bugging out, solid skills in and around the water are important. At the very least, you should know how to swim and be familiar with water rescue techniques. The ability to swim not only opens bug-out alternative routes, but it is also used as a life-saving skill. If you are already comfortable in the water, you can augment your skills by taking a lifeguard certification class.

SELF-DEFENSE

No matter why you choose to bug out, it is always a good idea to have a basic knowledge of self-defense. When it comes to civil unrest, you obviously need to protect yourself and your family, but you may also need those skills during natural disasters.

THREE SURVIVAL FITNESS TIPS

DON'T WORK OUT TOO MUCH IN THE BEGINNING

Physical fitness is important, but you should never overtrain. This can be dangerous, especially if you aren't in shape yet, but it can also cause you to lose your long-term motivation. Start out training about twice a week, and resist the temptation to do it more often. Even if you feel you can handle it, still don't push it. The anticipation of the next workout should build because it will let you go on for the long term.

DON'T UNDERESTIMATE WARMING UP

You should warm up at least fifteen minutes before any exercise if you don't want to risk getting injured. This seems like a lot of time to warm up, but it is important because it reduces your risk of getting sudden muscle spasms.

SMALL STEPS

You should always start small. Even if your first workup is nothing more than a thorough warm-up and a walk around town, it is enough. After walking for a while, you can start doing other exercises such as running, push-ups, sit-ups, squats and others.

When it comes to improving your health and fitness, every little bit counts. Just like stockpiling supplies, adding a little bit to your survival fitness program each day will continue to increase your conditioning. Even a simple half-hour walk each day will improve your chances of being better prepared than others.

Now that we know what you need to do to improve your disaster preparedness, let's take a look at your home and supplies.

GETTING YOUR HOME READY

When you make your home more efficient, you will increase your disaster preparedness and your chances of survival in an emergency. In addition, it will help you to save on electricity, water, and other costs. In a survival situation, your ability to power your home without reliance on the power grid, municipal water or other external resources can dramatically increase your chances of survival.

It can be overwhelming and difficult for a beginner to start making their home self-sufficient. You have a number of options, ranging from modern technology options to age-old methods. Let's look at some of the best solutions available to you for improving your home's energy, heating, water, and composting systems so you can have a truly self-sustaining home.

ENERGY SOURCES

When you want to find a self-sustaining energy source for your home, consider options such as solar and wind. However, each option may be available only to some preparers, so let's look at each one individually.

SOLAR

Solar has become a popular option since it is affordable and accessible. If you have the right conditions to capture enough sunlight, solar can be a great way to power your home. Solar power works by capturing the sun's rays with solar panels to generate electricity. Solar panels are found in two typical locations: on roofs and as standalone systems.

ROOFTOP SOLAR PANELS

When it comes to rooftop solar panels, positioning is very important. The panels should face within 90 degrees of direct sunlight and have full access throughout the day. This location obviously will change throughout the seasons, so you should calculate the ideal location for each month of the year and average the results to determine where to place your solar panels.

Another thing you need to consider is how much shade your roof receives and the pitch angle. If a part of your roof is shady, it will reduce the amount of energy you can harvest. Also, the pitch angle of the panels needs to be between 30 and 50 degrees.

Lastly, before you install any solar panels, you need to make sure your roof structure is sound enough to support the weight of a solar panel system. Your roof will also need about 300-500 square feet of unobstructed roof space. We went with solar panels on our roof 3 years ago. There are some great tax benefits to installing solar; just check with your local power company.

STANDALONE SOLAR PANELS

If rooftop panels don't work, you can consider standalone solar panels if your property is better suited to them. Standalone panels can be stationary or fitted with a solar tracker, which moves them with the sun to maximize power absorption. You can fit the panels with either single or dual-axis trackers; having both will increase the amount of energy captured by 25%.

PROFESSIONAL VS. DIY INSTALLATION

Professionally installed solar panel systems are a great option, but they are obviously more expensive. It can take several years before you can recoup your investment costs through energy savings.

If you can't afford to make the investment in solar panels, consider a smaller-scale system to charge batteries that can light small areas or power irrigation systems. If you are good with welding, you can even try installing your own solar panel.

WIND

Wind energy comes from turbines that provide an emission-free power source and can supply sufficient energy to power a moderately sized home under ideal conditions.

Before you install a wind turbine, the first thing you need to do is check local zoning regulations to make sure you can legally install a wind turbine. Next, you want to make sure your property is situated in an area that gets enough wind to produce sufficient energy for your home. A qualified manufacturer can help you determine the exact output you need, but most homes require around three to ten kW.

Wind turbines average 80 feet in height but can range between 30 and 140 feet. The height of your turbine will determine its productivity, especially if you live in a wooded area where the tree line may cause an obstruction. The diameter is often between 12 and 25 feet.

Wind turbines are also a steep investment of around $10,000-$70,000. It can take up to thirty years to pay off this amount with energy bill savings. Also, if you have a day without wind, you won't produce any power and will need a backup system in place. As a result, some people with wind turbines choose to remain connected to the local power grid.

If you want to remain completely off-grid, then you would need to store excess energy from productive days in batteries for later use. You can also reduce cost by building your own wind turbines, but I would suggest you against that.

ALTERNATIVE POWER SOURCES

If neither solar nor wind power works for your home, you can choose to get a backup power source that will make your home more self-sufficient in the event of a power outage or disaster. Consider a gas, diesel, or natural gas-powered standby generator with an automatic transfer switch already installed, this way if you happen to lose your electricity, the backup generator will automatically kick in and supply uninterrupted power to your home.

GENERATORS

Backup generators can be a reliable way to keep your household's power running during a storm or a power grid failure. When you choose a generator, there are two numbers to remember: the steady-state wattage, the amount of energy required to keep an appliance running, and the surge wattage, the amount of energy required to start up an appliance.

When it comes to lights, these numbers are often the same, but for larger appliances such as a refrigerator, the surge wattage can be nearly twice the steady-state wattage. You should consider both of these numbers when deciding which appliances to back up in case the power goes out.

WATER SYSTEMS

Securing your own water supply can be a bit tricky, especially if your home is hooked up to the municipal water system. Drilling a well is an obvious choice, but it isn't always the best option. If you can drill a well, consider installing a solar- or wind-powered pump to create a completely self-sustaining water system. If you can't drill a well, there are two alternatives to consider.

RAIN WATER

Rainwater is a renewable resource that you can easily collect in free-standing barrels or by linking directly to your home's gutter system. Unfortunately, water collected this way isn't safe to drink, but it can be used for other purposes, such as watering plants or even washing clothes.

WATER STORAGE TANK

A water storage tank can hold enough drinking water to sustain you during a short-term bug-in situation. However, you will need the space for this tank. If you are planning to bug out to an apartment without room for a storage tank, you can choose a sealed bathtub liner to use in an emergency.

HEATING SYSTEMS

Depending on where you live, the ability to heat your home during a crisis can be a life-saving measure. The safest and simplest option is to get a wood-burning stove, and another option is to use geothermal energy.

WOOD-BURNING STOVES

If you have never had a wood-burning stove system before, you should start small with just one stove until you master it and understand how it works; then you can add additional stoves for other rooms.

Modern stoves are very efficient and offer features that make it easy to regulate temperature and air intake. As a closed system, many models can be safely left on overnight.

Maintaining a wood-burning stove requires a constant stockpile of fuel (wood, in this case) stored in a dry, easily accessible area. Also, you will need to keep your chimney clean to ensure proper safety and function.

GEOTHERMAL ENERGY SYSTEMS

These systems use the heat energy given off by the earth below the frost line, making them effective at heating and cooling homes, no matter the climate. It operates on a closed-loop system, piping water from your home deep into the ground and back up again.

The earth's temperature is steady at 50 degrees F, so cold winter air can be heated and hot summer air can be cooled. Air circulates through ductwork and passes over water coils, where it is heated or cooled before circulating throughout the home. The system also has a compressor to enhance the heating or cooling effects by compressing or expanding the refrigerant.

While this system is highly effective, it is also expensive. The return on investment can be similar to that of solar panels, about ten to fifteen years.

COMPOSTING

While composting isn't a direct energy producer, it is a great way to conserve resources by turning food scraps and other organic debris into nutrient-rich soil for your garden. Your garden can then grow healthy food. Composting is inexpensive and very easy to do, whether you have many acres or just a few square feet. There is no reason you shouldn't start composting today.

OUTDOOR COMPOSTING

The most basic composting structure can be made from a single sheet of wire mesh by wrapping it into a cylinder and supporting it with wooden stakes. This simple design provides easy access to the soil at the base since you only need to remove the stake and open it at the side. It is also easy to relocate should you change your mind on the location. It can also be easily expanded if you need to increase your output.

The next step up from this mesh structure is to build a composting box, which isn't that much more complicated. The frame can be made of wood and lined with wire mesh on the sides. Pallets work well since they are already the right size and have slats for ventilation. Some designs feature a hinged gate on the upper front panel, allowing easy access to the soil.

VERMICOMPOSTING

Vermicomposting or adding worms to the process can increase the decomposition rate while also reducing odor. This is great for composting kitchen scraps or for apartment composting.

To set up this system, you need to use two plastic bins of the same size to create the perfect environment for worms. Drill holes in the recessed areas of the inner bin to provide drainage and aeration. Make sure the holes are small enough to prevent the worms from falling through.

For the lid, cut out a square and line it with window screen so oxygen and light can enter, orienting the worms and driving them down into the decaying material. Put a few rocks or wooden spacers in the bottom bin to keep them from sticking together and to promote additional aeration.

Now you can place the bin with the drilled holes inside the other bin. Place a layer of peat, newspaper scraps and wet cardboard as a healthy base to keep the worms' skin moist. Each day, add your scraps by burying them among the bedding material. Make sure you rotate the location, so you are burying scraps in a new area each day. You should also cut larger pieces to help them break down more quickly.

As the worms process food, they will produce droppings known as castings. These collect at the bottom of the bin and look like dark coffee grinds. There are plenty of nutrients in these castings that a plant can take up in its roots. This fertilizer will help you grow healthy, productive plants more effectively than chemical fertilizers, without any negative effects.

With just a little time and effort, you can make your home more self-sufficient. It may be a little costly to invest in self-sustaining systems for power, water, heat and composting, but it will pay off in a disaster scenario. Even if there is no disaster situation, you will be able to save money on your utility costs for years to come. Now, let's look at what you need to do regarding your water supply for disaster preparedness.

WATER PREPARATION

Water is the number one necessity in any emergency, whether it is short-term or long-term. The rule of thumb is to have at least 1 gallon per adult per day for drinking and hygiene. However, water is a heavy resource at 8.3 pounds per gallon. This will be heavy and bulky to move quickly, so you need to carefully consider your situation. If you aren't likely to have access to water, then you should carry it with you. However, if you have a nearby water source, you can use water purification as a solution. Water purification comes in many forms, including tablets, filters or sterilizing pens.

You should choose the best option for your situation and place it in your BOB, but also keep some ready-to-go water. The bottom line is to be aware of the resources in your area.

FOUR WATER STORAGE BASICS

In a crisis, having access to clean, drinkable water is a must, and your entire bug-out crew needs enough. Whether you are going to bug out or bug in, you will need to know a few fundamentals to ensure you are properly storing your water for long-term use and that you have enough to last you during a crisis.

HOW MUCH TO STORE

As we've already stated, you ideally need 1 gallon per person per day for at least 3 days. The average person needs 3/4 of a gallon for drinking per day and up to 1/4 of a gallon for hygiene and sanitation. If you are in a hot climate, nursing or ill, you are going to need more water. You can see how your water needs easily add up when preparing for a disaster.

The decision on how many days to store will depend on the type of emergency you are planning for. For example, storing water for a few days of emergency can be fairly simple, but planning for an extended period or a large group can be a bit more complicated. Before starting to stockpile water, you need to consider how much you need, for how many people and for how long.

CONTAINERS TO USE

There are two main ways you can store water. The first is to get pre-packaged water in traditional bottles or larger gallon bottles. This is a simple and inexpensive option. The second option is to use tap water since it is cheaper and just as effective. However, you should only do this if you have public tap water. If you use well water, you will need to filter and sanitize it first.

If you are going to bottle your own water, you can use plastic soda bottles, but plastic milk and juice containers aren't ideal. You can also use plastic containers built specifically for water storage and follow their directions for use. You should avoid using glass containers because they are heavy and prone to breaking.

STORING WATER

The best place to store water is in a cool, dry place. Basements are great if you have one. However, it is best to split your supply into different areas of your home in case one area is damaged or otherwise inaccessible after a disaster. It is a good idea to store water in every closet of your home, or at least in one closet on each floor.

EXPIRATION

If a container is properly sanitized, commercially bottled water is safe for up to six months. Most commercially bottled water has a use-by date printed on the bottle indicating how long it is safe to drink. If you are in doubt, you can boil the water and treat it with purification tablets before drinking.

Having access to clean and drinkable water is something many take for granted in first-world countries. In a crisis situation, finding safe drinking water becomes a priority for everyone. Whether you choose to buy commercial bottled water or make it yourself, the most important factor is making sure you have enough.

A little planning in advance will save lives and keep you effectively prepared for a long-term crisis. Now let's take a look at the other important preparation item, food.

FOOD PREPARATION

In a survival situation, food is the second most important requirement to stockpile for disaster preparation. Food needs to be well-kept, lightweight, and something everyone in your survival group is willing to eat. You won't be able to include fresh fruits and veggies in your stockpile since they don't store well, but you can grow these later in a long-term situation. The focus on stockpiling emergency foods is to keep your energy up with sufficient, as-healthy-as-possible calories.

Vitamin supplements store easily and are a good replacement for fresh fruits and veggies. You should also keep in mind any special dietary needs of your survival team members. If you have children, be sure to include baby food that is long-lasting, and if you have pets, make sure you stock up on their food as well.

It is important to know what types of food you can store and stockpile. Let's take a look at the best foods to store for a long-term disaster.

Canned Foods - Canned foods are obviously at the top of the list for several reasons. First, it has a good shelf life if stored properly. Second, most of the time it doesn't have to be cooked; you can just open and eat. Make sure you have a can opener on hand, or know how to open cans without one. There is a wide variety of canned foods to choose from, but ideally, you want to stick with something your family will eat. This can be the best way to get fruits and veggies until you can start growing your own. The shelf life of these foods can vary, sometimes lasting up to 3 years or more.

Dried Beans - Nearly any type of beans will do black, pinto, kidney, etc. Beans will last you for a few years, but pinto beans often last the longest. To maximize the time dried beans last, you need to store them in a cool, dark and dry place; ideally in vacuum packing. You can also choose to use canned beans since dry beans can become too dry to cook after three to four years, especially if something goes wrong in storage.

White Rice - Most recommendations are for brown rice since it has more vitamins and minerals and a slower absorption rate, so you have a steady flow of energy over a longer period of time. However, white rice is better for one important reason: a longer shelf life. White rice lasts about 4 years, while brown rice doesn't last much past 1 year.

Pasta - If you store pasta the old-fashioned way in Mylar bags with oxygen absorbers, then you can expect it to last up to fifteen years. Again, it should be kept in a dry, cool location away from pests. You should also store it in the freezer for four to five days before actually storing it to make sure you kill any larval eggs inside. If you don't do this, you may find little black bugs inside after a few weeks.

Dried Hazelnuts - Nuts are a wonderful source of protein and good fats. Hazelnuts have the longest shelf life of all, about two years. However, they do need to be stored at freezing temperatures.

Whole Grains - Whole grains are better to stockpile than flour. Flour only lasts a year, while whole wheat, rye, barley, etc., can last up to six months. If you store whole grains, be sure to have a grinder as well.

Dry Powdered Milk - This can be another good protein source, but it is better than other options like grains and mushrooms. Milk is a complete protein, meaning it also has the necessary amino acids that your body is unable to produce on its own in order to regenerate muscle.

Honey - a great item to stockpile with a nearly unlimited shelf life that can give you plenty of energy.

Peanut Butter - This is another great comfort food that can last ten years or more, but you have to do a few things first. You need to store it in a cool, dark place, but you also need to make sure you purchase a quality brand. When you open it, it should still be creamy and soft with no darkening.

Iodized Salt - Salt is important for the human body, and while a lot of foods have it, you should still have a supply of it on hand. You can store it in Mylar bags, but don't use O2 absorbers. Salt lasts forever since most bacteria and fungi cannot survive in it.

Sugar - As with salt, sugar can be stored in Mylar bags without O2 absorbers and lasts nearly forever.

Freeze-Dried Fruits and Vegetables - An alternative to canned foods. The idea is to remove all water from the food. To consume them, you need to add adequate amounts of water.

Cocoa Powder - This has a shelf life of two years, and you can do more than just make homemade chocolate. You can use it to make a variety of dessert options.

Pink Salmon - This has the best shelf life of all canned fish, nearly six years. If you don't open the can and store it in a cool, dark place, it will last a long while. If you do open the can, then you need to eat it within two to three days and keep it in the freezer.

Cooking Oil - The oils that last the longest in storage are those commonly used for cooking: sunflower, coconut, and extra-virgin olive oil. You can also use cooking oil as an emergency lighting source if needed.

Hardtack: a type of cracker made from flour, salt, and water. They are also known as sea biscuits or sea bread. Simply store the ingredients and make this whenever you want.

Spices and Herbs - Store these in Mylar bags with oxygen absorbers to add wonderful flavors to your food.

Jams and Jellies - It is sometimes said that these foods only last about a year, but if you seal and store them properly, they can last 5 or more years.

Food Bars - Food bars have a long shelf life and are a good option if you need to quickly throw something into your BOB. Some of these bars have a shelf life of five years or more. Energy and protein bars may give you the required carbs, but they are more expensive than peanut butter and often contain a lot of preservatives that aren't good for you. Therefore, they should be used only as emergency food.

Popcorn - a great comfort food everyone likes. It has a long shelf life when stored properly, except for microwave popcorn.

Fruit and Veggie Juice Powders - These come in a variety of flavors. While these aren't the real thing, they are better than nothing. When properly packaged and stored, these powders will last a long time.

Hard Candy - Stored in airtight containers, it can be a wonderful treat in a post-disaster situation. Don't store with an O2 absorber and keep them away from heat, light and moisture.

Baking Soda - Besides obvious cooking uses, baking soda has a million other uses. For example, mixed with a little water, it makes excellent homemade toothpaste.

Powdered Cheese - This is a great option with a shelf life of 10+ years.

Powdered Eggs - These come with a five-year shelf life, and you can buy them or make them yourself.

Vitamins: Use Mylar bags and O2 absorbers to extend shelf life to a couple of years. You should store each separately and make sure you rotate them regularly.

Coffee - Coffee will not only boost your energy but also make a great bartering item. Not all coffee lasts awhile. The best thing to stockpile is green, unroasted coffee beans in Mylar bags with O2 absorbers. Just make sure you have a means to roast and grind your beans.

Tea - Tea stored in a Mylar bag with O2 absorbers will provide a long-lasting beverage option.

Vinegar - This acetic acid has many uses. It can be a disinfectant, a grease remover, and a sore throat treatment, among other uses. Since vinegar is acidic, it has an indefinite shelf life.

Seeds - Seeds are going to be important when you grow a survival garden. However, you can't choose just any seeds. You need to choose ones that will grow in your region, and you'll need to know how to grow them. Gardening is a vital skill in a post-disaster situation.

Pemmican - a mixture of fat and protein from large game such as buffalo or deer. Traditionally, the fat and protein were dried, mixed and pressed. The shelf life will depend on storage conditions and the quality of ingredients. It doesn't need to be refrigerated or cooked, but it will last longer in a refrigerator. Due to its high fat content, it can go rancid over time.

Hard Liquor - Even if you don't drink, you probably want to stockpile this as it will make a great bartering item.

MREs - These are expensive and not quite as tasty and healthy as other options on this list, but they are good if you only want to build an emergency stockpile. However, beyond the 72-hour stockpile, you should focus on other foods from this list.

PET FOOD CONSIDERATIONS

You wouldn't starve in a post-disaster situation, so why should your pets? Pets play a huge role in our survival after a disaster. Cats will be able to catch mice to reduce disease; dogs will protect you from bad people; plus, pets can be a joy and keep you company.

STORING AND PREPARING PET FOOD FOR SURVIVAL

Are you stocked up with at least six months of pet food? Do you know what to do when the stored food runs out, and what you need to feed your pet? Thankfully, most pets require the same food groups that humans do, and providing pet food from scratch is a lot easier than you think.

CAT FOOD

Cats require less food than dogs and just a few basic ingredients. To make a week's worth of food for your cat, you need the following:

- ✓ 4 to 5 cans of tuna and 3/4 cup of cooked rice

- ✓ 3/8 pound chopped chicken liver or another meat substitute

- ✓ 4 sprigs of chopped parsley with stems removed

Access to tuna shouldn't be that difficult since tuna is already a food item commonly stored for disaster situations. Rice is also a popularly stored item. Simply drain the tuna and mix with the rice. Cook the chopped liver or other meat substitute, then add it to the mix. An option is to add the chopped parsley and serve. This will provide most cats with up to one week of food. When properly stored, it can last up to three months.

DOG FOOD

Dogs come in a variety of sizes and energy requirements. Make sure you provide enough ingredients to meet the daily serving size for your dog's breed. You will need the following ingredients:

- ✓ Six cups of water

- ✓ One pound ground turkey, chicken or meat substitute

- ✓ Two cups of brown rice, one teaspoon of rosemary and sixteen ounces of broccoli, cauliflower and/or carrots combined

Boil the water, then place the meat, rice, and rosemary in it. After it is thoroughly cooked, let it simmer for twenty minutes. Pour in the sixteen ounces of vegetables and stir for five minutes before serving. This will provide up to one week of food, depending on the dog. When properly stored, it will last up to three months.

FOOD STORAGE

Once you know which food items you want to store, you need to know how to properly handle them in storage. It is important that you have between three days' and a week's worth of food for each member of your household.

It is important to eat only foods people are familiar with and that don't require refrigeration or heating. Try to avoid eating and storing salty foods, as they can increase blood pressure and thirst. Make sure all food is given in small portions until it is consumed, to prevent leftovers without refrigeration.

There are some types of food that you should store in containers. You should never store food in trash bags, chemically based plastic barrels, empty paint cans or any other place that has had chemical contact. Containers meant for food storage will be shown on the label and are

BPA-free. If you are using previously used glass or plastic containers, you should make sure they are cleaned thoroughly to prevent any chance of mildew or another fungus. Never store anything in a box.

Most dried foods should be packaged and stored in tightly sealed, moisture-free plastic boxes or bags. You can also use food-grade biodegradable metal cans for dry foods like granola bars or nuts. Dried foods should have as little exposure to air as possible, since oxygen can cause them to spoil quickly. When storing food for the long term, it should be kept in a cool, dark place such as a cupboard or cabinet.

THE SURVIVAL FOOD PYRAMID

The survival food pyramid is a logical, simple and economical approach to stockpiling food. The top of the pyramid is reserved for stocking the smallest amount of food for the shortest amount of time.

This allows you to start with a cheap, easy goal and then work down from there. The pyramid prevents you from spending time and money on food preparation that might be useful but is pointless at this early start to your disaster preparation.

You can view the survival food pyramid here:

http://survivalcache.com/wp-content/uploads/2010/04/Food-pyramid.png

While there are no specific rules requiring you to follow this food pyramid, it can help you make the most of your disaster-preparation plan. Now you should have a good food and water stockpiling plan in place. Next, let's look at what you need to do to fortify and protect your home should you choose to bug in during a disaster.

FORTIFYING AND PREPPING YOUR HOME

No one has endless money to spend on disaster preparedness, especially when it comes to getting a return on investment, since they may never use some of the equipment. If you can't afford the equipment you need to bug out during a disaster, the next best thing is to fortify your home and bug in.

In addition to storing the basics of food and water, there are a few things you need to consider in order to fortify your home and make it safe to ride out the most post-disaster situation.

The first simple step you can take is to install upgraded solid-core doors made of either solid two-inch-thick wood or steel. You should upgrade the door jams to include latching faces screwed into the framing behind the door trim. While doing this, you should also install high-security door locks. Commercial-grade door locks provide an additional level of security for your home and are more difficult to pick.

Windows are also vulnerable to hazards such as flying debris during a disaster and to looters attempting to break a window after a disaster. One easy way to solve this problem is to re-glaze key windows with polycarbonate. This is the same kind of plastic used to protect bank tellers. This will stop most flying debris and even small-caliber pistol rounds.

Here is a YouTube video about re-glazing windows with polycarbonate plastic.

https://www.youtube.com/watch?v=tS9mjeReEl8

These are just a few simple improvements you can do to fortify your home in preparation for a disaster. Another way to improve your home in the event of a disaster is to build something called a Faraday cage.

PREPARE FOR AN EMP ATTACK WITH A FARADAY CAGE

An electromagnetic pulse or EMP may sound like a harmless event, but it is possibly the most devastating disaster that can happen. An EMP is essentially a burst of energy that can be either natural in the form of a lightning bolt or human-made.

Depending on the size and intensity of the EMP burst, it could potentially knock out electrical and information systems across a wide area. To prepare for an EMP, you need to know what it is and how you can defend against it.

WHAT IS AN EMP

An EMP, whether natural or human-made, can send out a burst of energy that knocks out power to the electrical grid. An EMP can have lasting effects from minor inconveniences to potentially sending the world back to a pre-communication technology situation.

WHAT IS A FARADAY CAGE?

There is a way to protect your equipment from an EMP event. The most popular option is to use a Faraday cage. This is a type of protective container with a conductive outer layer, often made of aluminum.

These "cages" serve as a shield, protecting any electronic devices inside from an EMP. The term "cage" comes from the fine metal mesh that is often used as a protective wall. However, research has shown that a solid sheet of metal is more effective.

You can build a Faraday cage of any size to accommodate any size object. Remember that an EMP can cause a voltage spike high enough to fry all types of electronic devices, including cell phones, computers, radios, and appliances. The only thing you need to have with a Faraday cage is to make sure it is thoroughly lined with a conductive material and has no gaps.

HOW TO BUILD A FARADAY CAGE

To protect large devices such as computers, televisions, tablets and appliances, you need a large shield room. You can do this by lining a closet with heavy-duty aluminum foil. You need to pay attention to how you place the foil around the door frame to ensure continuous coverage with no gaps.

Place cardboard on the floor of the room as you load items in, to prevent damage to the foil. You also want to look for outlets in the closet, make sure nothing is plugged into them, and ensure they are covered in foil.

If you don't have a closet or are in a prepping location that isn't your home, you can build a freestanding Faraday cage by framing a box with 2x4s and lining the outside with fine, conductive mesh. The openings in the mesh need to be small enough to prevent energy waves from entering.

In place of the mesh, you can also use sheets of aluminum or copper for shielding. Whatever material you choose to use, the coverage again needs to be continuous over the entire exterior or else the shielding won't be effective.

For smaller devices, you can use a shoebox lined with heavy-duty aluminum foil. Or simply wrap the device you want to protect in several layers of foil.

HOW EFFECTIVE ARE THEY?

The effectiveness of a Faraday cage depends on several factors. This includes the origin of the EMP, how far your cage is from it, and the types of radiation it emits. High-frequency waves require smaller holes in the meshing and short-range EMPs often have gamma rays and x-rays that can't be blocked by a single layer of heavy-duty foil. To fully protect against EMPs that come from radio-frequency weapons, you need thick sheets of metal.

So if you have any valuable information you want to protect, consider building your own Faraday cage. Now, the last thing I want to discuss with you is some tips for how you can prepare for a disaster, even if you live in a small apartment.

DISASTER PREPARATION FOR SMALL SPACES

By now, you're probably noticing the same common theme. I was seeing that disaster preparation requires a lot of room if you are going to stockpile appropriately. However, with 80% of the United States population living in urban areas, and this percentage being even higher in countries like China and Japan, there is a decent chance you live in an apartment or a smaller house without a lot of land or storage space. So how can you build a stockpile for an emergency when you can't even find enough room to hang your clothes? A little creativity is the key.

HOW TO MAKE IT WORK

To successfully store supplies in a small space, there are a few quick tips you need to know. Think about what things you have around the house that you never use. When you get rid of these extras, you will not only free up space for your stockpile, but you will also know what you can live without when a disaster happens.

PRIORITIZE

Next, apartment storage becomes all about prioritizing. Not all of your disaster supplies need to be stored in the same place. For example, a BOB needs to be pretty handy in a quick emergency. On the other hand, food or medical preparations can be tucked away without easy access, since you will only use them in a bug-in situation.

Consider what areas of your home have dead space. Most BOBs can easily fit under hanging clothes or next to the vacuum in a closet. When you see your kit, you will know every day where and how to get to it in the event of a quick emergency. Having it accessible will also encourage you to replace items with expiration dates and bring it out to practice skills on occasion.

For long-term disaster preparedness, you will need to look for hidden storage options. It is a good idea to break your stockpile up into smaller caches. However, each cache should be enough to hold you for a day or two.

MAKE THE MOST OF YOUR SPACE

Apartments aren't known for unlimited free space, so you are going to want to waste as little space as possible. Before you start stockpiling, plan where you want to keep everything so you stay organized and know where to put it.

If you are going to spread things around your apartment, it is important to keep an inventory with location and expiration date, so you always know where everything is and when it needs to be rotated. Consider some of the lesser-known storage spaces, such as the following:

➢ Under the bed

➢ Free-standing cabinets

➢ Overhead crawl space

➢ Behind furniture

➢ Overhead shelving

➢ Allotted storage space

➢ Sheds

➢ Medicine Cabinets

Again, it takes creativity to find places to store things in a small apartment.

THINK OUTSIDE THE BOX

If you have a really small apartment, consider whether or not you can use a private outdoor space for storage. While you certainly don't want to leave things piled up under a tarp, you can get small storage bins or outbuildings for relatively cheap, and they can greatly improve your space.

If you absolutely have no place to keep your stockpile, you can consider renting a storage container. This isn't an ideal option, but if it is your only choice, then you can do it. However, keep in mind the reality of your situation. In an emergency, how difficult will it be to get to your storage location and access your unit? You could consider storing other non-emergency items elsewhere and freeing up space in your home for emergency items.

If you are going to use a storage unit to stockpile emergency goods, then keep a few things in mind:

➢ Have a combination lock for increased security, even though it won't protect against bolt cutters.

➢ Carry and store stuff in bins or black garbage bags so people don't know what you are keeping in your storage unit.

➢ Store things in sealed plastic containers or 5-gallon buckets to keep out rodents.

➢ If possible, get a unit that is accessible from the outside. If not, be sure to choose a facility with manual doors so you can still gain access to your unit even when the power is off for extended periods.

➢ If your unit isn't temperature and humidity-controlled you should only use it to store non-perishable items and make sure everything is completely dry to avoid mold and mildew.

Finding ways to prepare for a disaster and stockpile is difficult when you live in a small place, but it's not impossible. You simply need to be careful in choosing what you store and use a little creative thought when finding storage locations. After all, the worst thing you can do is put off preparing for a disaster.

Now that you, your family, and your home are prepared for a disaster, let's take a moment to consider a few additional preps that will take you the extra mile in ensuring you are properly prepared.

OTHER CONSIDERATIONS FOR DISASTER PREPARATION

When it comes to preparing for a disaster, people pretty much know the basics, such as food, water, and supplies. There are a few areas that people don't think about as commonly. These three areas are financial, important documents, and location. Let's take a look at these to make sure you are properly prepared for a disaster scenario.

DISASTER EMERGENCY FUNDS

An emergency fund is certainly an individual decision. Financial experts vary greatly in their suggestions of how much money you should save. Some say $1,000, while others recommend no less than six months of expenses. Of course, the amount you are actually able to save will depend on your own financial situation.

Even if you aren't living paycheck to paycheck and can afford to set aside some money, there are other considerations, like where you should keep your money. When deciding how to prepare financially for a disaster, you need to consider the following.

ACCESS

After a natural disaster, you may not be able to gain access to a safety deposit box or an ATM. Therefore, if you have money stored away, be aware that your local bank can be damaged just as easily as your home. This is why some guides recommend keeping a few hundred dollars in cash in your BOB.

This will at least let you pay for a night or two in a hotel or for some food until you reach a place outside the disaster zone, if it is a small-scale disaster.

I have a friend who keeps real gold coins at home; he says it is easier to keep than cash. My theory is: always keep some cash handy, and if you must, keep a few gold coins as a safety cushion. But make sure to store them securely.

LOSS OF INCOME

After a natural disaster, it is also possible that your employer might experience severe financial difficulties.

That also means your employer may not be able to pay you, and you'll find yourself out of work for awhile.

This is why you shouldn't rely on your salary if a town is shut down due to an emergency. You should have at least one to three months of salary on hand if possible. You can also talk to your employer to find out what their policy is on paying during unforeseen events. This will help you determine what actions to take when trying to support yourself and your family during a disaster.

DON'T EXPECT HELP

There is a good chance that you'll receive some form of help from volunteers or a company after a disaster. This can come in the form of food, housing or money donations. However, you should never rely on this assistance. As you can see from past disasters, sometimes it takes relief workers awhile to get to affected areas and receiving help can take much longer than you expect.

No one wants to think about worst possible scenarios, but having money saved up in the event of a disaster is just as important as an emergency kit. A little bit of cash on hand will go a long way towards helping you and your family after a disaster.

IMPORTANT DOCUMENTS FOR EMERGENCY SITUATIONS

This is often one of the most overlooked aspects of disaster preparation; the collection and storage of important documents. Most people think of surviving a disaster and the immediate aftermath; they don't focus on rebuilding a normal life afterward. This requires having some critical documents. You don't want to have the frustrating process of trying to locate lost or destroyed documents.

WHAT DOCUMENTS TO INCLUDE

Planning and preparing for a disaster should include gathering essential documents. The ones you choose to include in your kit are up to you. However, some of the records you should keep include the following:

✓ Insurance policies, along with policy numbers and contact information for your agent or broker.

✓ Property deeds.

✓ Vehicle titles.

✓ Copies of social security cards and driver's licenses.

✓ Birth and marriage certificates.

✓ Passports or copies of passports.

✓ Bank account numbers and company phone numbers.

✓ Credit card numbers and company phone numbers.

✓ Stocks and bonds.

- ✓ Health insurance cards and prescriptions.

- ✓ Immunization records.

- ✓ Tax returns, both federal and state, for the last three years.

- ✓ Wills and estate plans.

You may also want to have a list of names and contact information for important individuals you may need to reach after a disaster. This can be family members, friends, doctors, lawyers, accountants and more. Depending on your situation, you may also need family photos, description of pets, veterinary information and pet medical history.

Some people will even take an inventory of their home, including description, serial numbers, dates of purchase, model numbers and value of items. This can help you reclaim items that were stolen or get payment for losses from insurance companies after a disaster. I always take pictures of every room showing all the furniture, electronics and even take photos of all my wife's jewelry, so in the event of a total loss, I can show them the picture as proof. I update the pictures once every year so they are current.

HOW TO STORE DOCUMENTS

Original documents can be kept in a safe deposit box, and then the keys can be kept in your BOB. You can also choose to keep your documents at home in a fireproof box, but these may not be as reliable. Another option is to scan important documents into electronic format.

The problem here is how to secure the document and still have access to them when you need them. You should also make copies and keep them in a sealed, waterproof pouch in your emergency kit. It is best to update your documents every six months.

Lastly, I know we've talked a little about location; but we haven't gone into depth about location yet. There are two things you need to consider: living in context to survival and where to bug out to in case of a disaster. So let's take a look at choosing these two important locations.

DISASTER LOCATIONS

Not everyone can simply pick up and move. However, if you are planning a move soon and really have a survival mindset; then consider choosing to move to a place with a good survival context. Or perhaps after reading this, you may find you already live in a good place with a survival context.

There are a few things you need to consider to make sure you are living in a location that has a good potential to survive after a disaster.

BEST PLACE TO LIVE WITH SURVIVAL CONTEXT

WELL DEVELOPED AGRICULTURE

This is important if you are going to need to grow your own food after a disaster. It is linked to the region's climate, the length of the growing season, and general soil conditions. The further south you live, the longer the growing season. This doesn't mean you can't live in the north and grow plants; it just requires more planning and possibly starting your plants indoors in a greenhouse. Then there are parts of the northwest that are very favorable for agriculture, such as Oregon and Washington.

WELL-DEVELOPED INFRASTRUCTURE

Most advise to avoid living in the city. A city relies too heavily on infrastructure. A major power outage lasting more than a day is likely to cause significant social unrest. However, if you live close enough to a city, you can still get the benefits of its infrastructure without having to be stuck in the city. For example, you have access to better health care and hospitals. The best safe distance from a major city is about an hour's drive.

CLEAN ENERGY

Thankfully, clean energy can be found pretty much anywhere. Solar energy tends to be more efficient near the equator. Southwestern states are good since they have less cloud cover during the year.

FRIENDLY PEOPLE

This can be subjective. In general, the South is known for having the friendliest attitude. The West often has a friendlier demeanor than the East. Also, the more remote your location, the more tightly knit the community, but it may take longer to be accepted by the local community; once they do, you become part of the family, so to speak. However, for some, this may not be an issue.

FREEDOM

This is important for those seeking greater self-sufficiency and homesteading practices. Cities and densely populated areas will have rules and regulations. However, there are also plenty of areas with few restrictions. You can examine the specific laws of each state to see which ones appeal to you.

ALTITUDE

This can be important depending on disasters in an area. For example, if you live along the seacoast at sea-level then you are at risk of flooding, hurricanes, and tsunamis. At high altitudes, you will have a shorter growing season and a colder climate. Weather patterns vary greatly based on altitude. It is best to consider the potential for disasters and choose a location and altitude that is comfortable for you.

CLIMATE

Climate goes along with altitude, but is just as important. Some people prefer certain types of weather and climate conditions. Along with personal preference, you want enough natural rainfall to sustain a summer garden. This rules out the majority of the west and southwest, which get their summer water from reservoirs. The best is a location with four seasons, as long as the winters aren't too long or harsh. You should also do your research and avoid areas with microclimates that differ from the regional climate.

PREDATORS / POISONOUS LIFE FORMS

In the west and northwest, you have to be aware of bears, mountain lions, rattlesnakes and poisonous spiders. But if you take common-sense approach and precautions, you'll be fine. The key is knowing your location and the dangers it presents so you can be cautious and prepare accordingly. In parts of the southern states, you have to worry about alligators. The central and northeastern parts of the US are likely to have the least dangerous predators compared to other areas.

FRESH WATER

This is perhaps the most important one on the list. Fresh, clean water is key to survival. This is found most often in mountainous regions. Obviously, the worst areas for this are the southwestern US and desert regions. Your best options are the northwest, southeast, northeast and some northern states. Ideally, you should get a location with a natural, year-round stream or a pond/lake.

POLLUTION

Pollution is typically concentrated at lower altitudes and in areas with high population density. Know what is upstream of the place you are looking to live and pay attention to air currents and water flow. All regions have prevailing wind directions. The jet stream typically blows from west to east. Discover the pattern in your area to know what is blowing your way. To avoid heavy pollution, you should stay away from cities and major transportation areas.

While there is no ideal or perfect place to live. You can always find a good reason to live or not to live in an area. When it comes to choosing where to live, you need to consider your own priorities.

However, not all of us can simply pack up and move to a better survival location. When the SHTF, we may be forced to bug out of our current location and head to a better one. If that is the case, you need to know how to choose a good bug-out location.

BEST BUG OUT LOCATION CONSIDERATIONS

Perhaps the most important tip for a post-disaster situation is to stay out of the cities. It is likely easier to survive in the wilderness than in an urban center. In both scenarios, you have to deal with wild animals. However, in the wilderness, you can have better odds of finding food, water, and shelter.

In urban areas, you will have to deal with the gang mentality that comes from no good sources of food, water, medicine and gas. So keep this under consideration when choosing a bug-out location.

While the wilderness may seem like a better option than the city or suburban areas, you shouldn't plan on it as your sole bug-out location. At some point, resources will become a source of competition when there are more people than the resources can supply. Unless you are a hundred or more miles from any major populated area, you are going to come across others. If you are going to bug out in the wilderness, make self-defense and protection a part of your plan.

If you are going to bug out after a disaster, consider how close your family and friends will be. If you are going to be near a major city and only have a handful of people in your group, it can get pretty challenging. You should make sure your bug-out location has a good network of like-minded individuals who can help you rebuild a community after disaster strikes.

No matter where you choose to bug out, you want to make sure the area can live off the grid for an extended period. Food, water, shelter, and defense are important. However, in the long-term, you are going to need to take electricity and other utilities into account.

Looking for these things will allow you to have a good bug-out location in mind. Then you can develop your plan for getting there in the event of a disaster. Now that we've discussed everything you need to do to be prepared, let's look at how you can do all this on a budget.

SAVE MONEY ON DISASTER PREPARATION

Disaster preparation isn't cheap. You're buying extra food and water, plus you're buying special gear for emergency kits. All of this can put a lot of strain on your wallet. This is why thriftiness is a principle of disaster preparedness. If you can live frugally and shop smart, you will be able to save money both on your disaster preparation and in your life in general.

There is a lot you can do to save money on disaster preparation, so let's take the time to see how we can help you save some money.

SPENDING HABITS

The best way to start saving money is to think about how you spend it. There are plenty of things you can do to alter the spending habits that will save you a lot of money, but still allow you to get what you need to get prepared for a disaster. Small adjustments in your daily spending can make a big difference in your overall financial health and free up more funds to invest in disaster preparedness.

CUT DOWN ON THE SMALL THINGS

❖ Prepare your lunches at home, so you aren't tempted to buy lunch out while at work.

❖ Eat before shopping at the grocery store.

e

- ❖ Quit smoking or other addictive habits.

- ❖ Stock up your fridge with groceries so you aren't tempted to eat out for dinner.

- ❖ Make your own coffee at home and bring it with you.

- ❖ Avoid buying things on an installment plan.

- ❖ Have a yard sale to sell off your old things.

- ❖ Cancel cable subscriptions and look for other online streaming devices where you don't have to pay each month.

- ❖ Buy quality clothing at thrift stores rather than brand name apparel at department stores.

- ❖ Repair worn clothes at a tailor rather than buying new clothes.

- ❖ Order online where you may be able to get better deals.

- ❖ Get a prepaid phone to save money over a contract.

- ❖ Avoid eating out unless it is a special occasion.

- ❖ Use coupons when you can.

- ❖ Walk when you can to improve health and save money on gas.

These tips are designed to help you reduce your spending costs. In addition to doing this, you need to shop smart to increase the savings you can enjoy.

Even after making the above changes to your spending habits, you may still not have much extra money to spend on disaster preparedness. Or perhaps you are already living so tight that you've already made these changes and are still having trouble paying for your basic needs. If this is the case, then the next step is to learn how to shop smart to save money.

Most people don't really pay attention to what they spend on groceries. They may pick a cheaper brand, but they don't take the time and effort to make sure they are getting the best possible deal.

However, when you're trying to buy a year's worth of food, even saving a few cents can really add up to huge savings. There are plenty of ways you can shop smart and save money, let's consider them.

COUPONS

Everyone knows about coupons, but often the items these work for aren't good survival food options. However, you can use coupons to get good deals on other survival products such as the following:

❖ Hygiene products

❖ Ziploc bags

❖ Batteries

❖ Pet food

❖ Insect Repellents

Save any coupons you find in the newspaper or mail and ask others for coupons they don't plan to use. You can even find a number of websites that provide you access to coupons you won't get in print ads.

BUY IN BULK

Again this seems like an obvious tip. However, what most people don't know is that you should start your buying in bulk with items you'll eat right away or within a reasonable amount of time.

At supermarkets, you often find deals on items in larger quantities. If you do this, you can store half in your stockpile as long as it's non-perishable and use the other half for your daily eating. You can also find some deals on bulk websites such as Groupon. If you cook, try making a large batch and freezing the leftovers.

GENERIC VS. BRAND FOOD

Try to buy generic medicines and food when possible. These often work and taste just as good, but come at a fraction of the price. A lot of smaller brands offer you better deals than the name brand products. Do your research to consider the best price to quality ratio.

ROTATE YOUR STOCKPILE

Try to never throw out any food. If something in your stockpile is going to expire, eat it and buy more to replenish it. This has the added benefit of getting you used to survival food before you have to rely on it. Plus, you can try different brands and flavors to make sure you are getting something you'll really be able to eat long-term.

BUY INGREDIENTS, NOT WHOLE FOODS

There are several advantages to this tip and one obvious downside. You are going to need more time to get these foods, and you are going to need the time to cook them. However, buying ingredients over whole foods comes with the following advantages:

❖ You save money because you aren't getting charged for making the product.

❖ It's healthier since you aren't getting preservatives and additives.

❖ Lastly, raw ingredients have a longer shelf life than cooked foods.

Raw ingredients also make for versatile cooking options. You can change up the seasoning and add new ingredients to boost the food's nutrients and flavor.

Another way you can save money is to do things yourself. Let's look at some projects that will help you save money in this area.

MAKE IT YOURSELF RATHER THAN BUYING

There are a number of things around the house you can choose to build yourself rather than buy them at a store and save a lot of money. It can also be a fun activity and a chance to teach your children some valuable skills.

You can also apply this to home repairs. Learn the basics and fix your own home. This not only allows you to learn new skills, but also helps you save money by avoiding the cost of hiring someone else to complete the repairs.

Make your own soap or laundry detergent. Often, $30 of raw material will make you something that costs you about $80. You will also be saving money by not having to travel to the store.

GROW YOUR OWN FOOD

Starting a garden has many benefits. You grow fresh fruits and vegetables that provide a healthy food source. Plus, you will save money by buying food at a store. Lastly, you can be sure you are getting organic and fresh produce that hasn't been genetically modified.

REPURPOSING

Another way to save money is to repurpose items. Look around at what you have and think of ways you can repurpose an item you may not use as much. People in third-world countries have long learned to do without many of the things that many of us in first-world countries consider necessities.

The reason for this is that they use what they have, even if it isn't specifically designed for the job. This doesn't mean you have to hoard everything, but simply hold on to items if you think you can eventually have another use for them.

SWAP, BARTER, EXCHANGE, SCAVENGE

Use your network of individuals that you've built up when developing a disaster plan. You may have a farmer who raises organic beef that can give you a special price on meat.

Talk with your family and friends about swapping clothes. Most people have good clothing they never wear, which may work for you.

Often, other disaster-preparers understand the importance of being prepared and will be willing to trade with you. If you have something they want, they'll trade with you so everyone can be better prepared. This can also give you some training in bartering, which will be important in the post-disaster situation.

Scavenging goes along with repurposing. We live in a disposable society, and most people throw away decent items all the time. Drive around the neighborhoods on trash day and see what people have set out for trash. You'll often find something you can repurpose.

You can also consider trading your labor for something you need or can use. If you can save people money on labor costs, they are likely to agree to your deal.

Lastly, consider scavenging wood and using it to build a variety of things. Many times, you will find people giving away wood pallets for free, and online you can find thousands of DIY projects that use pallet wood. Go to smaller businesses that are less likely to have a deal with a company and ask to take their wood pallets.

There is no shortage of ways that you can acquire items needed to build and set up your bug-out location or fortify your home for a bug-in situation. Lastly, let's look at the 80/20 Rule that will help you efficiently stockpile your disaster supplies.

THE 80/20 RULE TO PREPPING

WHAT IS THE 80/20 RULE?

The 80/20 Rule is: Aim to achieve 80% of the results with 20% of the work, but the last 20% of the results will take 80% of the work.

This rule applies to your BOB. Let's take a look at how this can work.

WHAT TO PACK

When it comes to packing your BOB, you likely already have most of the supplies at home. Basically, all you need to do is put the items in a bag. So, 80% of your BOB gear is already in your home, such as the following:

✓ Socks

✓ Underwear

✓ Shirts

✓ Pants

✓ Food

✓ Water

✓ First aid supplies

✓ Medications

- ✓ Flashlight

- ✓ Lighter/Matches

- ✓ Cordage

- ✓ Comfortable shoes

- ✓ Pocket knife

- ✓ Duct tape

- ✓ Floss

- ✓ Super glue

- ✓ Tinfoil

- ✓ Trash bags

- ✓ Ziploc bags

That would leave you needing to buy at least 20% of items such as the following:

- ✓ Radio

- ✓ Tent

- ✓ Survival knife

- ✓ Paracord

- ✓ MREs

- ✓ Water filter

- ✓ Dust mask

The weight of your BOB is one of the main factors that determines how far and at what speed you can bug out in an emergency. A heavy BOB causes you to burn more energy and thus need more food and water to survive. And after hiking for a while with a heavy pack, your mental fatigue worsens. However, you can also use the 80/20 Rule to help you get rid of a lot of weight in your BOB.

First, comfortable shoes are important when bugging out in an emergency. However, they should be on your feet so you need to wear them rather than storing them in your BOB and adding weight.

Second, water is vital to survival. However, you don't need to bring a week's worth with you. If you know how to find and purify water, which is an essential skill you should learn, then you can get by with just a 16-ounce bottle of water. This can take a lot of weight out of your pack.

Food is also important. However, the goal isn't to have as much food as possible; rather, it is to have as many calories as you can. So, it is best to focus on small, calorie-dense foods that keep well.

Lastly, you want to consider your shelter. If you are going to bug out in a non-urban environment, then your shelter is very important. When it comes to reducing your shelter weight, you want to consider two things:

1. What do you have, and what material is it made out of?

2. What can you change or leave behind based on your specific situation?

Consider using just a sleeping bag or tarp instead of a full tent. Or, in our book on survival gear, we will discuss a bivy bag, which is similar to a personal tent and very lightweight.

SPACE

After you've gone through your bag to reduce its weight, you'll have more room for other essential items. Look at the largest items in your BOB and consider whether you really need them or if there is a smaller alternative. If you have excess space, leave it rather than filling it with non-essentials; you may need to scavenge along the way and have some place to put what you find.

All right, now let's say you still can't do any of the above to get a BOB started, and you still want to prepare for a disaster. Then let's look at some free options you can do to start a BOB.

21 FREE DISASTER PREPARATION ITEMS

1. **Work Out** - We've already discussed the importance of fitness in disaster preparation and how you can develop a good fitness routine. Getting in shape and starting a fitness routine doesn't cost a thing.

2. **Foraging** - No matter what type of area you live in, you can forage. As long as you aren't trespassing and you know what plants to eat, you can start practicing your skill of foraging while adding some delicious edible plants to your next salad, all for free.

3. **Make a Home Inventory List** - There are probably a number of items in your attic, garage, basement or closets that can work great for a post-disaster situation. Make a home inventory list, or at least consider what items you haven't used in awhile. If you haven't used an item in a while and it serves no useful purpose post-disaster, consider selling it. However, you would be surprised to learn that nearly 80% of items in your home can be repurposed to help you post-disaster.

4. **Bartering** - Bartering doesn't have to be a skill you only use after a disaster. Use bartering today to get the supplies you need. Barter for supplies in exchange for your skills, and you'll get something for free while practicing a useful skill.

5. **Make a Plan** - Know what disasters are likely to happen in your area. Use the information at the

beginning of this book and develop your emergency plan so you know what to do when a disaster hits.

6. **Practice Drills** - Once you have an emergency plan in place and everyone knows what to do, consider doing some practice drills. Practice bugging out, first aid, bugging in and home invasions, to name a few. This will give you an excellent opportunity to be ready for a disaster.

7. **Learn a Foreign Language** - Is there another language commonly spoken in your area? Are you planning to bug out to a location where the language is foreign? Consider using a free online website to teach you a foreign language, so you can learn an additional skill for a post-disaster scenario.

8. **Find Holes in Your Plan** - If you've been prepping for a while, then take the time to sit back and go through your emergency plan again. Look for areas that are missing or places that have changed and need updating.

9. **Use Coupons for Free Stuff** - There are plenty of print and online coupons that can allow you to get stuff for free. It may not be major survival gear, but it will at least get you some general household goods to stock up on for an emergency.

10. **Harvest Rainwater** - First, make sure this practice is legal where you live. You won't need an entire system right away, but if you have a few barrels,, you can start gathering some water. Then use it to water your plants, do dishes, flush the toilet, etc.

11. **Free Items from Fast Food Restaurants** - Most fast food restaurants give free plastic utensils, napkins and small packets of salt and pepper. If you eat at these locations, get a few extra of these items to save with your stockpile.

12. **Reorganize** - If you want to eventually expand your survival stockpile, you're going to need extra room. In the meantime, take the time to reorganize your home and make room for your emergency supply.

13. **Dig a Place for Your Cache** - You may not be able to do this until you actually have the stockpile complete, but consider at least finding a location where you can dig in your backyard and hide your cache.

14. **Prepare a Safe Room** - Keep some of your gear inside and try to reinforce the location where you have it. However, use only the supplies you have on hand so you don't have to buy anything.

15. **Label Everything** - If you are eventually going to expand and increase your stockpile, make it easier on yourself by labeling what you already have. Or you can even pre-label containers with what you plan to get eventually, so you'll have a designated space for everything once you do.

16. **Plan Bug Out Routes** - As we've already discussed, you want to have multiple bug-out routes planned. Take the time to sit down and map them out along with some landmark locations, so you'll be adequately prepared.

17. **Train Your Dog** - If you have a pet, consider starting dog training on your own. You don't want your dog to be uncontrollable when chaos starts happening. So go online now and learn training tips for free.

18. **Practice Being a Gray Man** - Post-disaster, the best thing you can do is blend in with those around you. Practice this today so you can be prepared. I'll cover this subject more in the third book of this series.

19. **Take Free Classes** - There are plenty of online and offline classes that you can do for free. These can range from survival to homesteading, and all will include valuable tools and information to prepare you for a disaster.

20. **Practice Your Skills** - Buying items can be expensive, but learning how to survive or how to use equipment doesn't cost you anything. As we've discussed earlier in this book with a list of survival skills, take the time to start learning some.

21. **Start Reading** - Reading is free, and you can do it through your local library. There are plenty of survival books to read at the library or articles online. Either of them can provide you with valuable information.

So we're getting down to the last of it. We've discussed what you need to do to prepare, what supplies you need to get and how to save money. Now let's look at where you can get your supplies.

WHERE TO BUY DISASTER PREPAREDNESS GEAR

Bartering is becoming more common in today's society, especially as the economy starts to struggle. Bartering for survival gear is happening both in person and online. If you want to swap gear or barter for survival supplies, there are four places to consider shopping.

AMISH AUCTIONS

This can be a fun and interesting experience if you want cheap barter options. This is a good choice for farming, livestock raising and off-the-grid living tools and products, along with some household items. One of the largest Amish auctions occurs in Ohio Amish Country for five straight days.

YARD SALES

This is an excellent source for great deals on a wide variety of items. These typically occur more often during warm-weather months, but now the internet has made virtual yard sales popular year-round. When visiting a yard sale, you can always try bartering with the seller to see if you can get a better deal.

CRAIGSLIST

This is a great website to find yard sales, but it also provides lots of other resources. There is a section where you can find free items in your area, and a barter section offering plenty of items you can use for disaster preparation.

FLEA MARKETS

There are numerous indoor and outdoor flea markets across the country. You can often get some excellent deals at flea markets, and most sellers will be willing to barter with you.

What if you prefer to do your shopping online? After all, there are some great deals you can find online. So, let's take a look at what you need to do to get some great deals online.

HOW TO SHOP ONLINE

There are plenty of great deals online. But have you ever bought a great deal only to be disappointed when it arrived? For every good deal online, there are nearly three times as many dishonest sellers offering counterfeit goods.

Buying anything online, let alone survival gear, is a constant challenge. You also have the near-impossible task of determining an item's quality and practicality.

You often have to make a blind choice between a low-cost bargain with unknown quality and spending a lot of money on top-end equipment from a reputable local shop. Either option requires some level of risk. Let's look at how you can minimize this risk when buying survival gear online.

KNOW YOUR OPTIONS

Most survival gear can be divided into at least two groups: heavy versus light, expensive versus cheap and do-it-yourself versus premade. Knowing the choices you want to make is something you should learn through research of the gear you are looking to buy.

When you understand all the options available to you, you will know whether the price is fair or too good to be true. It can also help you to know which options or features are worth paying for and which you can do without. Be sure to carefully consider all the pros and cons available to you to make the decision.

WEIGHING YOUR OPTIONS

When you can weigh the options of your gear, you will be able to buy something that meets your survival needs. Consider the time you put into your research a valuable investment, since it will pay off when you get the right gear the first time. This is better than buying several types to find the one that works best for you. Carefully research what survival problems you are likely to face before you buy your gear.

KNOW WHAT QUALITY LOOKS LIKE

Before you shop for gear, know what the best option looks like. If you want the best deal possible, then you need to know what a great item and seller looks like. When you have this knowledge, you will be able to quickly tell a good deal from a bad one. When you can identify quality gear and sellers, you save time, money and unnecessary headaches. Here's what you need to be on the lookout for.

RECOGNIZING QUALITY

A good seller will have their phone number and some form of physical address listed on their website. When someone has spent the time and money to set up a phone line, it generally means they take their business seriously. It often means they care about their customer service enough to let people talk to a person rather than a computer.

Lastly, it means they are confident in the quality of their gear and don't expect many angry phone calls.

Quality sellers are also going to have good user reviews. Research has shown that 70% of Americans look for product reviews before they make an online purchase.

Sellers who allow customers to leave feedback and make it visible to the general public are an excellent way to generate positive buzz about their products. It also proves the seller's confidence in the quality of their products and their belief that others will share their positive reviews. On the other hand, a website with poor quality gear is going to hide its reviews.

Even if you aren't shopping for name-brand products, shopping at a website that does sell name-brand products is a good option. A website that advertises recognizable brands it has in stock is obviously sourcing quality gear. This also allows you to comparison shop when you want to get the best possible deal on quality gear.

KNOW WHAT BAD STORES LOOK LIKE

Once you know what a good website looks like, you also need to learn the warning signs of a bad website. Here's what you need to be on the lookout for.

While there are deals out there, you are generally getting what you pay for. So if a price is too good to believe, it probably is. If something is too cheap, it is often full of junk that doesn't really perform well. A price that is too cheap can also be an indicator of a knockoff.

If the website is full of low-res pictures, it often means the seller is trying to hide poor workmanship. This means they don't care about their customers and just want to take your money. Quality sellers will provide large, high-res images so you can look at the details of what you're buying.

Tricking you with a list of included items is a common practice on poor websites. They often want to inflate the number to make it seem like they are sending you a large number of items. For example, a poor-quality seller will count every Band-Aid in the first-aid kit as an item, so you get a 100-piece kit, whereas a quality seller will advertise the entire first-aid kit as one item. Remember, the key is to focus on quality and not quantity.

When you follow these rules, you can be sure you are buying quality survival gear online. Remember, you want to first determine what is important to you to save time, money and problems. Then keep an eye out for indicators of good and bad sellers. This can ensure you don't get ripped off when buying your survival gear online.

This pretty much covers all the ways you can save money when getting prepared for a disaster. The last thing I wanted to discuss in disaster preparation is how to practice survival drills at home.

SCENARIOS TO PRACTICE FOR YOUR SURVIVAL DRILLS

One thing that has been covered a few times in this book is the importance of practicing your emergency plan and running drills to prepare for what to do in an emergency. Let's take a closer look at how you can do this.

NATURAL DISASTER DRILLS

Natural disasters can strike at any time, whether you're completely ready or not. These would be events such as tornadoes, hurricanes, and earthquakes, to name a few. To practice for such events, you will need the following:

✓ An emergency plan

✓ Your emergency packs

✓ All family members

✓ Cell phones or other methods of communication

Set a specific time for the drill to begin. Make sure everyone has a copy of the emergency plan in hand, and that it fully details how the family will handle the emergency, how they will communicate after leaving home, contact information for people outside the affected area, and where the family will meet.

Give a five-minute warning before starting the drill. Shut off the main power to the house. Turn cell phones to airplane mode or off. Sound an alarm to start the drill. Make sure the drill starts and finishes on time.

During the drill, you should ask yourself the following questions to evaluate its success:

❖ How did the family do?

❖ What were the weaknesses during the drill?

❖ Did any equipment have a malfunction?

❖ How long did the drill take?

❖ Was anyone frustrated?

❖ What improvements can make the drill better?

Remember, the more you practice, the better and quicker everyone will become. Make a note of any mishaps that occur during the drill so that you can correct them. Since time is of the essence and you want to be ready as soon as possible, make sure you practice regularly. It is also a good idea to do a few drills at night.

If possible, consider an unscheduled surprise drill to assess the plan's strengths and weaknesses and identify any faults.

FIRE DRILLS

A house fire can also occur at any time. There are many potential causes of residential fires. No matter what the cause, the effects have a major impact on those who live there. Prepare for a home fire by practicing drills, so you and your family will know how to react. For these drills, you will need the following:

✓ The emergency plan

✓ Fire alarm

✓ Handheld Stopwatch or watch

✓ Your emergency packs

✓ All participating family members

✓ Cell phones or other communication methods

✓ Towels or dust masks

As with a natural disaster drill, set a specific start time. Again, make sure everyone has a copy of the emergency plan. A fire drill plan should include a way for the family to exit the house safely and successfully, since getting out is the main priority. Review the plan one more time with everyone before starting. Make sure everyone agrees on the predetermined meeting point to gather after evacuating the home.

Give a five-minute warning before starting the drill. Sound the fire alarm or another type of alarm. Rally your family, coach them out of the house via the planned route, and make your way towards the meeting point.

Encourage everyone and keep them calm while at the meeting point. Record the time it took for your family to complete the drill.

After the drill, ask yourself the following questions:

❖ How long did it take to complete the drill?

❖ How did the family do?

❖ Were there any weaknesses with the family during the drill?

❖ Was anyone frustrated during the drill?

❖ How did the kids handle the drill?

❖ Did everyone take the drill seriously?

❖ Can improvements make the drill better?

❖ Would the family perform as well in an actual fire?

Since fires can happen at any time and often occur quickly, it is a good idea to practice several times a month until everyone is comfortable with the plans. Make sure you quickly correct all issues with equipment or attitudes.

If you don't acknowledge any issues, this can cost lives. As with natural disasters, you should do several nighttime drills. Families that are caught unaware or unprepared in the middle of the night are the ones most likely to die in a fire. An unscheduled, surprise drill will test everyone's strengths and weaknesses, so you can identify any faults.

No one likes to think of an intruder entering the safety of their home. This comforting thought process can put people in a vulnerable position. However, it is still a good situation to practice. For this drill, you will need the following:

✓ The emergency plan

✓ A safe room or escape plan

✓ A safe room

✓ Weapon

✓ Nylon rope or other means to escape out a window

✓ Meeting point for the family

✓ Cell phones

Intruders tend to strike at night, so you should ideally set the drill for late at night or early in the pre-dawn hours. Make sure everyone in your family knows the emergency plan and understands the importance of speed and efficiency.

Start the drill with an alarm, the sound of breaking glass, or a door being forced open. Your family should recognize these sounds as their signal to take action. It is key that your family knows how to perform the drill in silence while heading for the safe room. The safe room should be farthest from the front door to put the greatest distance between you and the intruder. Time your family as they make it to the safe room. Once inside the safe room, lock the door.

Another option is to do the drill at night. Have two evacuation points planned. If you have a two-story home, have some family members on the top floor and some on the bottom floor. If you have children, you should practice the drill regularly, so they don't become overcome with fear when the real thing happens. Have the family evacuate and meet at the designated meeting point.

After the drill, ask yourself the following questions:

❖ How long did it take to finish the drill?

❖ How did the family do?

❖ Did all the family members know where the safe room was?

❖ Did the family evacuate safely according to the evacuation plan?

❖ Are there any improvements that can be made?

❖ How can you guarantee the safety of your family if the real thing happens?

❖ Are you prepared to use a weapon to protect your family?

Home invasion drills are important but understand that it can be very stressful for family members. The thought of someone coming into your home and harming your family takes a toll on your emotions. Be ready to address emotional and mental issues during and after the drill. Practicing at night is important, but you can practice during the day as well.

ACTIVE SHOOTER DRILLS

These drills aren't exactly for the home, but they are important to practice or at least discuss these days when a shooting event can occur at any time, anywhere. An active shooter drill will ensure your family is ready and knows what to do if they face an active shooter. For this drill, you will need the following:

- ✓ Your emergency plan

- ✓ Family members participating in the drill

- ✓ Room to simulate a school room or a workplace

- ✓ Audio recording of gunshots

- ✓ Stopwatch, timer or watch

- ✓ Prop gun, if you want

- ✓ Cell phones

Active shooters can happen anywhere at any time, so you should practice these drills at various times and set them in different settings. Start the drill by playing the audio-recorded gunshots to unsuspecting players. The goal is to startle the family into action. Play a variety of recordings, alternating sounds. The aim is to make the drill as realistic as possible, so you can create a sense of fear.

Take note of how your family reacts. Note who makes themselves an easy target. If a family member follows the plan correctly, they should be able to disappear before your eyes. How long does it take family members to get out of sight?

After the drill, ask yourself the following questions:

❖ How long did it take people to get out of sight?

❖ Did anyone make themselves an easy target?

❖ How well did everyone perform?

❖ What are the odds of survival based on how everyone executed the plan?

Active shooting incidents are rare, but they are happening with greater frequency. You should practice these drills at least once a month and go over the plan with each family member individually. No two people react the same way, so you should tailor your discussion to each individual.

Remind everyone that the key to surviving an active shooter situation is to stay low and out of sight while trying to get away from the shooter.

These are just a few drill suggestions you can use to simulate real-world emergencies. You can come up with other drills based on what happens most often in your area, or change things up to suit your individual needs.

If you have disabled or infirmed individuals in your family, include them in the drill, so everyone knows what needs to be done. If you have pets, practice evacuating with them as well. This will acclimate the pets to their carriers and the process, so you won't be hunting for your animals and shove them in carriers at the last minute when a real situation occurs and every second counts.

LAST WORDS

As I said in the beginning, this book along with the next two are merely the course I taught for last two years to various groups of people that wanted to learn how disaster survival. I have deiced to break this course down to 3 books, so it is easier to consume.

The next book in this series is all about the **Ultimate survival gears**, their use and what is good and what is not. Since I am not as a pro on that subject, I had Henry Miller a good friend of mine to help me talk about what and how gears work. So in the next book, Henry is my co-author or co-pilot as I like to call him since in real life he is a commercial flight instructor.

The last book or the 3rd part of my survival course is all about what and how to survive a real disaster, so it is essentially all about what you should do **during and after** a major disaster.

I wanted to thank you for buying my book; I am neither a professional writer nor an author, but I am a professional hiker and a bushcraft survival coach. I wanted to share my knowledge with you, as I know there are many people who share the same passion and drive as I do. So, this book is fully dedicated to you.

Despite my best effort to make this book error free, if you happen to find any errors, I want to ask for your forgiveness ahead of time.

Just remember, my writing skills may not be best, but the knowledge I share is pure and honest.

If you thought I added some value and shared some valuable information with you, please take a minute and post a review on my behalf wherever you bought this book from. This will mean the world to me.

If you need to get in touch with me for any reason, please feel free to email me at BushcraftTrainer@gmail.com

Good Luck and Thank You!!!

APPENDIX 1: ACRONYMS

SHTF - S*it Hits The Fan

Bug Out or Bugging Out - Leaving a home as a result of disaster

Bug In or Bugging In - Fortifying and staying in your home until everything's corrected.

BOB - Bug Out Bag, a backpack filled with essential survival items should you need to leave your home in a disaster.

INCH - I'm Never Coming Home, an oversized Bug Out Bag that is designed for wilderness survival for two to three months.

COMSEC - Communications Security, not letting others know about your disaster preparation or telling as little as possible.

OPSEC - Operations Security, what you will do in an emergency and how you will use your resources.

www.ingramcontent.com/pod-product-compliance
Lightning Source LLC
Chambersburg PA
CBHW060305290526
45789CB00001B/406